AN
ILLUSTRATED HISTORY
OF
SMALL BOATS

At the Height of the Storm.

An illustrated history of
SMALL BOATS

A history of oared, poled and paddled craft.

PERCY BLANDFORD

SPURBOOKS LIMITED

Published by
SPURBOOKS LTD
1 STATION ROAD
BOURNE END
BUCKINGHAMSHIRE
ENGLAND

SBN 0 902875 51 5

*Printed in Great Britain by
Biddles Ltd., Guildford, Surrey.*

CONTENTS

LIST OF ILLUSTRATIONS

All the drawings in this book are by the author. All the photographs are by him, except for those indicated below. Many of his photographs were taken at the National Maritime Museum, Greenwich and at the Exeter Maritime Museum, whose co-operation he gratefully acknowledges. Plate 68 was supplied by Inflatable Products Ltd., and life-boat photographs and engravings are reproduced by courtesy of the Royal National Life-boat Institution.

INTRODUCTION

That often misquoted remark by Water Rat about the joys of messing about in boats was obviously directed at the smaller type of craft. Many of us get a lot of enjoyment out of paddling a canoe or kayak, rowing a dinghy or skiff, or poling a punt. The satisfaction comes from making progress through the water by our own muscle-power, without the aid of mechanical power or even the wind on sails.

In the earliest times man had to find how to drive himself when sitting on a raft or log. Different people devised different ways. Some developed skills in using a paddle while facing forward. Others produced more power by using an oar while facing aft. Some used both methods as well as a punting pole when conditions suited. As skill in boatbuilding progressed there came multi-oared craft, in which the oarsmen worked in powerful teams as propulsion machinery.

For a long time sail, if it was used at all, was complementary to rowing and only used in a following wind. Even with the coming of sailing ships and then mechanical power, manual power still had a place in smaller craft. When transport on land was hazardous or impossible in bad weather because of the state of the roads, goods and people could be transported by water. Watermen were numerous and an important part of the community.

The craft and the techniques of propelling them have progressed over the centuries so that modern rowing, paddling and poling craft are very beautiful and effective examples of craftsmanship. In these days of mass-production, when most people have to be content to only make one step in the production of an article, boats are still mainly the products of loving craftsmanship, often seen right through from start to finish by one man.

In these pages I have looked at the development of manually-propelled craft throughout the centuries and in many parts of the world. This adds up to a comprehensive survey of how men have found ways to master the rivers and seas in craft they have designed and built themselves. In some cases incredible journeys have been made in the most unlikely craft. I have found a fascination in compiling this book. I hope the reader will find it similarly absorbing and rewarding.

Percy W. Blandford

CHAPTER 1

Primitive craft

One of early man's first discoveries, that wood would float, must have led him to experiment with ways and means of using wood to keep himself afloat. He would have soon discovered that sitting astride a log was a very unstable way of making progress, so from that stage the trade of boatbuilder evolved.

Primitive peoples in widely different parts of the world used their own ideas, yet there are many similarities, although they could not have known about each others' activities.

There are two broad divisions in the ways of dealing with the unstable log problem. One is to alter the shape of the log itself and hollow it so the user can sit inside. This has developed into the mono-hull boat, which is the normal type in most waters of the world. The other way is to join several logs and make a raft. Apart from the basic raft form, this has developed into the catamaran and other multi-hull forms.

If a log is split down the middle and hollowed, it still has an unstable semi-circular form if nothing is done about it. The cure is to flatten what will be the bottom of the hull, so the cross-section is more of a D form. Where a mono-hull canoe is being made, this is the shape to aim at. Primitive man must have come around to this by experiment.

Until the coming of metal tools, hollowing would have been done very laboriously and slowly with stone axes and flint knives, probably aided by fire. As the use of metals developed, nearly all workers made a type of curved adze to use for chopping out the inside of a log canoe. This was supplemented by a deep gouge or broad chisel, which was the same sort of cutting tool, but intended to be held on the job and hit with a mallet.

The obvious way to form the canoe was to hollow it symmetrically and point the ends, but because of the grain formation, this meant chopping from the ends towards the centre and there was a risk of a split developing and opening through an end. Some Pacific islands had dug-out canoes with open sterns. The problem of keeping the water out was solved by sitting a woman in the end. An open-ended hull is easier to chop out, and easier to empty after pulling ashore.

Dug-out canoes are still used and even where civilization has made itself felt there are still men able to make boats in this way.

Birchbark canoes were possible in the northern part of America, but the trees that yield a suitable bark did not grow in what are now the Southern states of the USA, so Indians there made dug-out canoes. The Florida cypress provided an easily-worked wood for the Seminole Indian boatbuilder. Similar craft were made by other native

Plate 1. A Nigerian dug-out, propelled by either pole or paddle.

craftsmen in central and the northern parts of South America.

Some dug-out craft were given a V-shaped bow *(Plate 1)*, but those intended for rivers, particularly if rapids were involved, had raised narrowed ends. Solid log craft of this type were quite large on Brazilian rivers, and to keep them reasonably light craftsmen worked patiently to finish the hulls to quite thin sections.

Trees grow largest and straightest in tropical forests. Consequently the most suitable trunks for making log canoes are found in the countries bounding the equator. This means that the natives of Central America and the Caribbean islands had the opportunities in the American continent, while there is a belt across Central Africa and another across South East Asia. Large dug-out canoes are found in all these areas *(Plate 2)*.

Even today, many of the working craft of West Africa are dug-outs. These are sea craft, launched through the surf, and used for fishing. People along this coast depend almost entirely on fish for protein in their diet. The dug-out log canoes are 25ft (7.5m)-30ft (9m) long, with a beam of about 4½ft (1.3m). Most of them are built from African mahogany—often a selected tree is brought from a hundred miles inland. They are nearly all entirely dug-out, with no built-in plank sides.

West African dug-out fishing craft were intended to be propelled by six or more

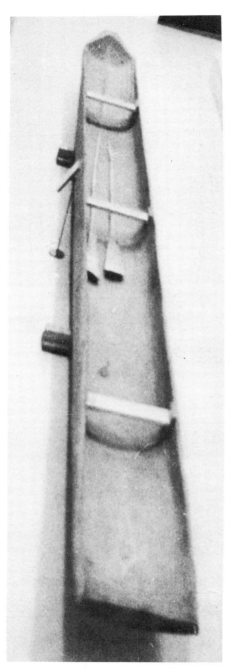

Plate 2. A dug-out, called a piroga, from Brazil. This one is 34ft long.

paddlers. Today it is estimated that there could easily be 50,000 dug-out canoes still being used as work boats, but large numbers of them now have outboard motors, mounted in wells through their bottoms. Although pointed, rather than spoon-shaped ends, are favoured, the bottoms are given considerable rocker to raise the ends above the water, as an aid for getting through surf.

In most places off the West African coast, fish are plentiful and easily caught. This may have encouraged a rather casual attitude. Getting any boat through surf is difficult, and African fishermen often let the boat go so that it probably capsized and tipped the load of fish into the surf. They then swam ashore and collected the fish from the beach, then righted and dragged up the boat for further use.

Even the North American Indians were not entirely committed to birchbark. Some very large dug-outs were used in the north west, and on large lakes in their territory the Iroquois Indian used dug-outs, keeping their bark canoes for streams and for raiding.

Those workers who favoured the raft idea, used several forms, depending on local materials. The Australian aborigine still makes a simple raft of mangroves held together with vines. Bamboo does not grow to a very large diameter, but its form of many airtight sections makes it buoyant. Fijians, and others, lashed together rafts of several layers of bamboo, so even with the lower layers submerged the upper layer gave a reasonably dry platform. Balsa wood is one of the lightest woods, although it has little strength. Where it grows, mainly in tropical America, it can be used for rafts, and this wood provides the local natives with a means of getting afloat. The Spanish invaders of Ecuador found the natives using balsa craft for coastal trade.

3

Plate 3. A model of a proa, showing an outrigger hull.

Thor Heyerdahl used the idea for the *Kon-Tiki* expedition and sailed 3,700 miles across the Pacific on a balsa wood raft.

A raft is satisfactory if all that is needed is something that will float and go with the current. Its confused underwater form is the reverse of what is needed in any sort of boat that is to be propelled and driven in a chosen direction. Because of this, native craftsmen in many places obtained stability by using two logs as hulls, kept apart by crossbars. Early versions were propelled by paddlers sitting on the logs. Later craft had a platform on the crossbars to carry cargo. The two logs were then hollowed so paddlers could kneel inside. As they obtained stability by being united to each other, there was no need to give each individual log a stable underwater section.

A true catamaran has both hulls of the same size. Many native seamen, like some of their successors today, favoured a main hull with another serving only to provide stability. The large main hull provided all the accommodation and carrying capacity. The other hull was much smaller and probably solid. The main hull was paddled as a canoe, but there always had to be sufficient load towards the other hull or float to prevent capsizing the other way. In some craft a man was poised on the crossbars and he moved his weight in or out according to the amount of stability needed.

Such a craft is known as a 'proa' in the Pacific islands, particularly when sailed as well as paddled *(Plate 3)*. In many places, because of the disposition of the islands and the steady prevailing wind at about right-angles to the usual course between islands, a proa was double-ended and the sailing rig reversed for a return journey. The float was always towards the wind and the best sailing was with the float just skimming the water. A crewman was always ready to move his weight out towards it to prevent a capsize if the wind freshened.

Having floats both sides of the main hull is now called a 'trimaran.' It had some use for primitive craft and was particularly useful for larger ones. Rowing was never an activity of Polynesian, Melanesian or other native seamen. They used a single-bladed paddle. While a large crew might paddle a long low canoe, there would come problems of stability as attempts were made to make it even larger. A mono-hull would have to be broader and deeper, but by adding floats in a trimaran form a long, low, easily-paddled hull could be made in a large size, while being made safe with the outrigger floats. The crew then had the benefit of the speed which comes with the length of any hull.

Hollowed log canoes were developed in many places, but the most adventurous users were natives of the Pacific. There seems to have been a universal urge to explore. Just as the monks from Ireland almost certainly crossed the Atlantic in skin boats, many South Sea Islanders braved the unknown in their rafts or dug-out canoes. The Maoris of New Zealand came thousands of miles from islands of the Polynesian group, many hundreds of years before Captain Cook reached New Zealand.

The largest dug-out canoes, particularly those used as mono-hulls, had their sides built up with planks. The logs then become the base on which was built something very like the conventional boat of northern waters. Some of these craft had timbers or frames crosswise inside, so the design was even closer to plank-built boats.

The largest dug-outs were war canoes. Their successors may still be seen. The royal state canoes of Thailand still have signs of their origin. Maori war canoes have survived. Native chiefs had their special canoes in which they were paddled by a large crew on state occasions.

In some places the would-be seaman had no worthwhile trees. There are pictures showing Egyptians using inflated cow skins. The idea is still used on the Sutlej River in the Himalayas. Several pig or cow skins are inflated and lashed together with a platform on top to make a raft—the precursor of our modern inflatable dinghy.

There are some craft which come between boats and rafts. Although boat-shaped, they rely on the buoyancy of the wood from which they are made, rather than on watertight joints. Typical is the Lobito Bay raft boat *(Plate 4)*, which is an African boat built of poles lashed together in a boatlike shape with a high bow and a transom. There is a theory that the shape of Chinese junks evolved from raft boats similar to this.

Reeds may seem an unlikely boatbuilding material, but where nothing more suitable could be found they were used. Reeds bundled together in a sufficiently dense mass will float for some time before becoming waterlogged. They will not stay buoyant indefinitely, but in a warm climate a reed boat may be used for a few hours, then hauled ashore before it soaks

Plate 4. A Lobito bay raft boat, built of poles lashed together.

up so much water that it would sink. After draining and drying, it can be used again. Such is the theory of the reed boat.

Bundles of reeds were fashioned into a bowl-shaped raft to keep a Middle-Eastern fisherman afloat for a few hours. High in the Andes on Lake Titicaca at 12,000ft fishermen make craft of more boatlike shape, using long bundles of reeds, tightly bound around, then these sausagelike bundles were grouped together to make a hull with its ends turned up. This was poled or paddled and some simple sailing was managed with a reed mat sail.

On Lake Chad in the upper part of the Nile Valley reed boats have been used, even from before recorded ancient Egyptian days.

According to Egyptian records these craft were developed into better boat shapes. The material was the papyrus reed which is extremely plentiful there still. These reeds were tightly bundled, apparently in much the same way as was done until recently by the South American fishermen of Lake Titicaca, then built into a boat shape. The estimated life of such a boat was four to six weeks.

According to Egyptian records some of these boats were 50ft (15m) long, but this unlikely material, which must have soon become a soggy mis-shapen waterlogged mass, would have been rather frustrating to any conscientious boatbuilder, although Thor Heyerdahl recently made a considerable voyage across the Atlantic on a reed raft.

Plate 5. A Batina coast 'Shasha,' made from palm fronds.

Plate 6. In the 'Shasha' a platform keeps the occupants above the water.

Plate 7. Canoe in the floating market at Bangkok, Thailand.

Plate 8. Fishing boat in Thailand. The bowman is ready with his net.

Although not strictly a reed boat, the Batina coast 'shasha' was made almost entirely from the central stem of the date palm fronds, with a few stiffening twigs. Trees of this part of Arabia were regarded as too valuable as shade for people and animals to be cut down for boatbuilding. The raftlike hull was held together by lashings and had a platform to keep the occupants above most of the water. These unlikely craft *(Plates 5 and 6)* were, and still may be, found used for fishing several miles offshore.

In eastern countries boats developed through dug-outs and rafts to shapes comparable to western boats, but where western craftsmen paid much attention to finish, their counterparts in the east appeared to be happy with craft that were functional without much regard to appearance. They also had the advantage, in many cases, of using woods which were durable in wet conditions without paint or other treatment. Many hardwoods can have a long life without special protection. Teak is one eastern hardwood of this type, now prized for boatbuilding in the west.

In Thailand (Siam) the shape used for craft from tiny one-person canoes to quite large manually-propelled boats, was evolved from dug-outs, although most are now built-up. Characteristics are very little freeboard amidships and high ends having straight, instead of pointed decklines *(Plate 7)*. The high ends and short waterline would make the boat easy to turn, although not so easy to keep on a straight course, and give extra buoyancy in the ends when dealing with waves or stepping ashore from the bow or stern. Propulsion is still by long single-bladed paddles, held by both hands around the shaft *(Plate 8)* instead of with an end grip, in the western style.

CHAPTER 2

The mechanics of manual propulsion

Primitive man sat on his raft or log and used a stick as a paddle, with very little blade area and very little leverage. All of the power came from his arm muscles and his stroke was quite short. He probably soon discovered the advantage of a broader and flatter surface to push against the water and something like the modern paddle shape was born.

Of course, the amount of blade area effects the amount of effort needed to move it, so a 'low-geared' paddler, who favoured powerful slow strokes might favour a fairly large blade, while a 'high-geared' paddler would achieve a similar amount of progress by quicker strokes with a smaller blade.

Sitting and using the arm muscles only is inefficient mechanically. The stroke can be lengthened by kneeling. The North American Indians discovered this and arranged their canoes so that they knelt in the bottom with their thighs supported by a thwart. It is only in modern pleasure canoes that seats have been fitted. From a kneeling position there can be a reach forward and press back, using the muscles of the back and thighs to increase power.

Even greater power can be obtained by kneeling on one knee, while the other leg is bent, with the foot forward *(Plate 9)*. This allows the hands to gain more leverage by being further apart and a greater swing with the use of more muscles, but is a rather tiring stance to keep up for long. Islanders in the Pacific used this method for getting the maximum speed in their large war canoes. A racing canoeist adopts the same stance today.

In a large canoe with many paddlers, the turning effect of each person only pulling on one side was balanced out, but such a canoe usually carried a steersman, who used a large paddle as a rudder. With a smaller number the turning effect has to be controlled. With only two paddlers, paddling on opposite sides does not balance out as the turning effect of the man in the stern is more than that of the man in the bow. With only one man in the canoe paddling on one side, there is obviously a considerable turning effect if nothing is done about it.

Canoe paddlers in many parts of the world developed what is now often called a 'J stroke.' This is a method of using the paddle as a rudder without slowing the canoe or the need to change sides. As the paddle is drawn aft it is turned towards the end of the stroke so that the driving side turns outwards. The amount of kick outwards before withdrawing the paddle from the water is regulated to keep the canoe straight or put it on the desired course.

A large number of special paddle strokes were developed, especially by the North

Plate 9. *Propelling a canoe with a single paddle. Note the stance and J-stroke, which keeps the canoe travelling in a straight line.*

American Indians, particularly for controlling their canoes in rapids. These strokes are being used and further developed by canoeists competing in slalom today.

The value of a double-bladed paddle does not seem to have been realized by many primitive paddlers. Only the Eskimos were regular users of it in their kayaks. Sitting in a kayak and making strokes alternately on opposite sides makes keeping a straight course easy. Using such a paddle over a long period is less tiring than making the same progress with a single-bladed paddle. As with the single blade, a paddler makes as long a stroke as reasonably possible. Not only is there a pull with one arm, but there is a thrust forward with the other. If the arms are widely-spaced there is considerable leverage on the blade in the water.

In a canoe or kayak the paddle is not connected with the craft in any way. Consequently the effort expended is only converted to forward progress of the canoe or kayak through the paddler's body to his contact with the hull. This can put considerable strain on body muscles which are not directly employed in the action of paddling. Thrust is transmitted by the single-bladed paddler through his knees or feet and by the double-bladed paddler through his contact with a seat, but more by the thrust of his feet against a stop and partly by his knees thrusting against or under the cockpit coaming or special knee grips.

The size and blade area of a paddle or oar depends on many factors, including the available material. A large blade area on a long levering shaft should produce the most power, but there is a limit to what effort a man can exert. People vary in their 'gearing'—

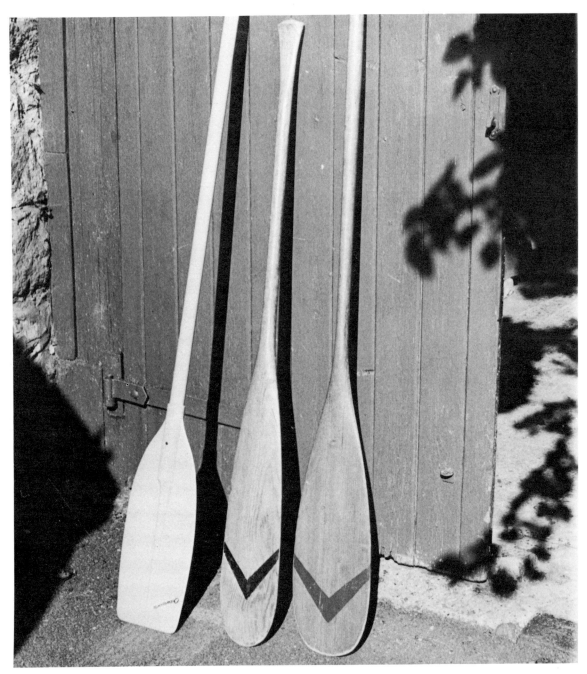

Plate 10. Three typical paddles. The left-hand one is aluminium and plastic. The centre is traditional beaver tail form, and from a single piece of wood. The right-hand one is from a laminate using resin glues.

some are better at long slow strokes, while others favour quicker and shorter strokes—the former being better with the longer leverages and greater blade areas.

In general, all over the world, paddle blades are not far from 7in (18cm) wide and 20in (50cm) long, where the material available does not set other limits. The length of a single-bladed paddle depends on the freeboard of the canoe and the height of the paddler, but 5ft (1.5m) to 7ft (2m) is usual. Some paddles have straight tops, but the Red Indians had shaped grips. The American beavertail form of blade *(Plate 10)* seems most efficient. Single-bladed paddles were not normally spooned, as either side might have to be used in special strokes. Spooning has been tried for modern racing paddles and the blades are much more spadelike than the graceful general-purpose paddles.

Double-bladed paddles, as used by the Eskimo often had quite narrow blades, in line with each other, but this was mainly due to limitations of material—mainly driftwood. Modern double-bladed paddles have large light spooned blades in most cases. The favoured wood is Sitka spruce, which is lightest and has adequate strength. As these paddles have to be supported as well as used without contact with the canoe, weight reduction is important. As a double-bladed paddle may be between 6ft (1.80m) and 8ft (2.4m) long, it is usually arranged with a joint at the centre for easy transport. This also allows the blades to be set in line with each other or at right-angles in either direction *(Plate 11)*. As twisting is done with one wrist, and not all paddlers use the same one, it is necessary to set the blades the right way if spoon blades are to come right *(Plate 12)*. With flat blades, where either side can be

pulling, the direction of twist does not matter.

There is an advantage in making paddle or oar blades thin, mainly for lightness, but this may leave end grain weak with a tendency for the blade to split. This has been got over in many ways. Single-bladed paddles are not usually protected and ash oars resist splitting. There may be bands of copper tacked around near the ends *(Plate 13)*. Better oars, certainly those used with smart inland craft, have usually had copper tips. Some Eskimo paddles had bone ends. In more recent times, plastic tape has been used instead of copper.

One advantage of paddling is that the operator can see where he is going, but his effort is not being used in the most efficient way. The effort of which a man is capable is better converted into forward progress of a boat by pulling one or a pair of oars. There is no evidence of who discovered rowing, but its use has been known in many parts of the world since prehistoric days. However, stories of multi-banked oars can be shown to have been mechanically and physically impossible past a certain point.

The big advantage of rowing over paddling is that the levering action against the water is transferred to forward motion of the boat via a fulcrum. The oarsman, facing aft, pulls against this fulcrum and levers the boat forward. The amount of leverage that can be applied is governed by the length of oar that can extend inboard of the fulcrum and the distance between a reach forward with arms extended and a pull back with the arms bent that a man can manage.

The obvious fulcrum or pivot for an oar was a notch or hole in the side of the boat, but an alternative was one or two 'thole pins' standing above the gunwale. A pair of pins served in the same way as the notch, but with a

Plate 11. Centre joint of double bladed paddle.

Plate 12. A spoon blade paddle with the blades at right angles.

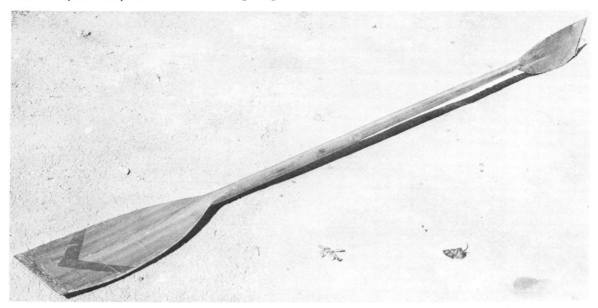

single pin there was a retaining rope loop or the oar had a hole to fit over the pin. Of course an oar with a hole cannot be feathered, but this type is still found on some coastal craft and is still favoured for boats on Lake Windermere.

In naval language a 'rowlock' has always been a notch in the side of the boat and a metal fitting in a socket was a 'crutch,' but to most people today a metal or plastic pivot for rowing is a rowlock (English) or oarlock (American). Most rowlocks have been made horseshoe-shaped and the oar pulled against the higher leg. A complete circle is found in the USA, but is not popular elsewhere.

One man pulling two oars having their fulcrums on the gunwales is limited to the lengths of oars that meet in the middle. In some craft a little more leverage is obtained by letting the oar grips overlap. In a racing boat or light pleasure boat, which has a narrow hull in any case, the rowlocks are held outboard by outriggers *(Plate 14)*.

The limit of a man's reach can be extended by giving him a sliding seat. This also allows him to use his leg muscles, as his legs straighten when he is pulling the oar. This arrangement, which allows the longest stroke and the greatest power, is used in modern racing craft, but was not used or known in older boats. Consequently, the size of oars which could be used was limited by a man's reach from a fixed seat, using his arms and body, with little benefit of reach attributable to his legs.

With his feet against a rest or 'stretcher' and his seat moving on wheels, a man can use most of the muscles of his body and achieve the maximum amount of forward progress of which he is capable, as his feet provide the point against which he thrusts while he gets

Plate 13. Copper tips on typical oars. The top one is a sea-oar.

15

Plate 14. Victorian skiff with rowlocks on out-riggers. Note fixed thwart.

the strongest pull into the grip of the oars to lever the boat along.

There can be an increase in leverage in smaller single-banked (one man per thwart or rowing position) boats, by sitting at the side opposite to the rowlock. This was done in some early craft up to about 30ft (9m) long and can be seen in Naval whalers today. Larger craft have to be double-banked.

If there is to be more than one man per oar, the one furthest inboard has the greatest movement. The maximum size of oar is governed by the distance he is capable of moving the end of the oar shaft backwards and forwards. Galleys had up to four men per oar. The one nearest the side of the ship had much less work to do than the one furthest inboard.

An oar extends outboard usually between two and three times the amount it projects inboard. The lower the rowing position, the shorter need be the oar. If one bank of oarsmen is put above another, the upper oars have to be considerably longer, and even if the ratio of the outboard length to the inboard length is increased, the physical movement of the upper inner man is just about stretched to the limit. It is unlikely that there were many successful ships with three banks of oars and drawings of ships with more than three rows of oars extended each side can only be accounted for by the imagination of the artist, rather than to the facts he is supposed to portray.

Most oars have been straight-bladed. Some have been given weight inboard of the rowlock to provide a counterbalance to the great

Plate 15. Typical blade shapes. The top is a straight oar, used for yacht's dinghies. The centre is spoon shape, suitable for inland river craft. The bottom is a modern double-bladed veneer paddle, for a canoe.

length outboard. Even in the more utilitarian workboat oars graceful shapes have usually been achieved, as they make for lightness and reduced load on the oarsman. Sea oars have been made of ash, where this was available. Although rather heavy, this flexed and oarsmen liked the 'kick' at the end of a stroke, which this springiness gave. In an attempt to reduce slip in the water, some light pleasure boat oars have been given spoon blades usually with a stiffening ridge at the centre. Theoretically, they scoop water rather than push it aside *(Plate 15).*

Of course a boat can be rowed by standing and pushing on the oars. This lacks the power of a pulling oarsman, but it does allow the oarsman to see where he is going. No doubt, because of this the method is used in Mediterranean harbours, where a man alone in a boat has to thread his way through moored craft. The Venetian gondolier has his own particular way of rowing with a single oar while facing forward. His technique has something in common with the Red Indian's 'J' stroke, but directional control can also be attributed to a certain extent to the shape of the boat, and this is dealt with in Chapter 5.

Modern oarsmen and double-bladed paddling canoeists make much of feathering their blades—the blade in the air is turned horizontal and offers less wind resistance. There is no evidence of this being used in

Plate 16. Typical inland punts unchanged from Victorian days, and propelled by poles.

18

earlier days. Modern kayak-like canoes were introduced in the middle of the nineteenth century by 'Rob Roy' McGregor. For the whole of his life paddles were used with their blades in line. It was not until the early 1920s that the value of having the blades at right-angles was appreciated. Feathering was by dipping one wrist while going forward. The feathering of oar blades was introduced at about the turn of the century, when lighter and narrower racing craft became possible and the feathered blades skimming the water also provided stability.

A boat is pushed forward by the reaction to the blade of the paddle or oar pressing aft, but as water is a far from solid substance there is considerable slipping and the actual amount of forward progress compared with the distance the blade goes aft is quite small. Obviously, if the depth of water allows the bottom to be reached, a pole can be used to press against it and forward progress should be much better for each stroke taken.

The Red Indian stood to pole his canoe up rapids. The technique has been used for other native craft. The pole is dropped near vertically in placid water or at a slight angle aft in moving water, then the hands quickly walked up it to thrust the canoe forward, followed by a quick recovery to repeat the operation before the current has forced the canoe back. This method is seen today with Thames and other punts (Plate 16), where the pole is used at one side of an aft deck. Straightness of course is achieved by a slight outward thrust to counteract the deviation caused by the thrust being off-centre. Some regattas include poling canoes and special narrow racing punts.

Larger craft are poled while walking along a side deck. On shallow rivers, such as the Irrawaddy, in Burma, cargo boats are moved this way, from side platforms. On the Norfolk Broads this is called 'quanting.' The boat is steered by its rudder, but the man using the quant drops the end to the bottom while he is near the bow and walks along the full extent of the side deck while leaning against the top of the pole.

Some near round craft, such as a coracle, were and still are propelled with a single-bladed paddle. The technique is what a yachtsman would call 'sculling over the bow.' The spadelike paddle is used at the side towards which progress is intended and manipulated so that strokes are made to alternate sides in quick succession. The effect is to pull the craft in a slightly zigzag way in that direction with alternate strokes cancelling much of the sideways thrust.

Sculling over the stern is a basically similar method designed to push the boat forward. This was used with quite large sweeps to move big laden craft in restricted places. Nowadays it is more often seen as a means of propelling a small dinghy (Plate 17). The oar is used in a rowlock or a notch in the transom. The blade drawn across at about 45 degrees sets up a reaction that tries to push the boat partly to the side, but more in a forward direction, because of its underwater shape. The blade is reversed, but still with the same side aft, and a pull the other way cancels the sideways thrust set up, but adds more to the forward thrust, so the boat is driven along.

As can be seen, the blade has to be turned through about 90 degrees. This is about the limit of movement of a wrist, which bends forward on one stroke and backwards on the other.

Many other ways of using manual power

Plate 17. Sculling over the stern, from a post-war chine dinghy.

have been tried. There have been lifeboats equipped with handles and foot pedals driving a propeller. Hand-operated side paddle wheels have not been found useful for anything except children's pleasure boats on a pool. At one time canal boats were taken through tunnels by the crew lying down and 'legging' through—walking on the roof or side of the tunnel. In the days when roads were often so bad as to be impassable, goods were moved on rivers by teams of men hauling with ropes. Where the bottom or bank is out of reach and the boat has to be moved manually, nothing has been found better than rowing to make the best use of the power that a man is able to exert.

A skilled oarsman or paddler can maintain his course by varying the blade pressure, but with large crews some sort of separate steering is needed. The Vikings and many others steered with one or two large oars or sweeps, trailed over the stern. In more recent days, western and many other boats have been fitted with rudders, usually hung with pins, called 'pintles,' fitting into sockets, called 'gudgeons.' The most popular method of steering has been a tiller, although the coxswain has been able to sit facing forward more satisfactorily if he had rope yoke lines, taken to each side of a yoke across the rudder head. Most primitive craft with rudders have followed one of these methods, but unusual thought has gone into the rudder of the Dubai shahoof *(Plate 18)*. This Arabian fishing craft has a balanced rudder blade, with part of the blade area forward of the pivot line (as used on some high-speed modern power craft), and a tiller pointing aft, controlled from a rope at each side. The bottom of the rudder is pulled forward into a groove by a rope. This can be released to allow the rudder to float free and avoid damage if the boat runs aground.

20

Plate 18 The rudder arrangement of a Dubai Shahoof. This can be propelled by oars or lateen sails.

CHAPTER 3

British and related skin boats

When the Romans invaded Britain in 55 BC they found the local people using skin boats. They were sufficiently impressed to record some details. Despite the passing of over 2,000 years, skin boats of basically the same design and construction are still being made and used today.

The modern name 'coracle' may not go back very far. The Welsh, who have more affinity with the Britons of Roman times than the Anglo-Saxons, called the craft *corwg* or *cwrwgl*. The latter form was corrupted into the English *coracle*. The oldest Welsh spelling was *corwc*, and this was used for skin-covered seagoing boats as well as river craft. In this form it is obviously related to the Irish (Erse) *curach* or *curragh* (the modern spelling).

English coracles were essentially inland river craft. The size and design were governed by the size and shape of an opened out cow or ox hide, which could then make a covering without joints that would leak. The framework inside might be considered to be a basket of interlaced strips of wood. Sizes varied according to hides available, but would not be more than about 5ft (1.50m) long, 3ft 4in (1.01m) wide and 15in (38cm) deep. In this size boat the normal crew could only be one, but load-carrying possibilities were considerable. The late Harry Rogers of Ironbridge, one of the last Severn coracle makers, ferried four

men across the river with them standing facing inwards around him while holding each other's shoulders *(Plate 19)*.

Coracles still in use on the Welsh rivers Towy *(Plates 20 and 21)* and Teifi *(Plate 22)* are probably nearest to the original concept, except that they are covered with tarred canvas instead of hides. They are used mainly for salmon fishing, usually by a pair of coracles having a net between them. The one man in each coracle uses a paddle long enough to reach his shoulder. By wrapping his arm around the paddle and resting the upper end on his shoulder he is able to scull single-handed and handle the net with his other hand.

There are two ways of making a coracle framework. Ash or willow strips may be thrust into the ground and bent over to shape, interweaving as they go. After the framework is built up, weights placed on the centre press it down to give the necessary flat stable bottom. Alternatively the framework is made the right way up, with the strips interwoven and pegged on the ground then their ends pulled up. In both cases the original strips would have been full round, then with the coming of iron tools they would have been cleft strips. Today they are sawn strips. Green wood bent to shape and left will settle into the forced shape. The top edge was then held by twisting

Plate 19. An Ironbridge coracle, the last of the English coracles. Note the spade-like paddle.

strips, like the edge of a basket and the covering sewn or thonged to it.

A board across the centre forms a seat and braces the whole framework. In the Teifi coracle the sides are pulled in above the seat. This may give some clearance for using a paddle at the side, but it results in an ungainly appearance. Coracles on other Welsh rivers tend to be more shapely and some can only be built with use of more modern tools, but the Teifi coracle can still be built with only the simplest tools, so is probably nearest to the original British form. As there are more coracles in use on the River Teifi than elsewhere it looks like being the type to survive longest.

The use of coracles has died out within living memory on the rivers Wye and Usk. There is evidence that at Bewdley, on the River Severn, coracles of the Ironbridge type were in use until the early part of the twentieth century and a family named Tolley were still using damaged raw hides from a local tannery as skins towards the end of the nineteenth century.

While fighting another Roman army in Spain in 49 BC Julius Caesar was faced with the loss of communications by bridges destroyed by floods. A translation of his own account of the affair gives us the first positive evidence of skin boats:

'When the affairs were in this unfavourable position and the bridges could not be repaired, Caesar ordered his soldiers to

23

Plate 20. A Teifi coracle of cleft wood.

Plate 21. A towy coracle.

Plate 22. A Teifi coracle, showing the thwarts and paddle.

make boats of the kind that his knowledge of Britain a few years before had taught him. First the keels and ribs were made of light timber, then the rest of the hull of the boats was wrought with wickerwork and covered with hides. When these were finished, he drew them down to the river in waggons, and transported in them some soldiers across the river, and on sudden took possession of a hill adjoining the bank.'

These were obviously not river coracles, but must have been quite large rowing boats, as waggons were needed and many soldiers were transported. This points to the Britons having larger coastal hide-covered craft. Pliny, in the first century AD, makes several references to boats of osier covered with hide being used by the British to transport tin probably from the Isle of Wight to Cornwall. He also refers to writings of the historian Timaeus concerning these British craft. Timaeus died about 256 BC, so British skin boats have an extremely ancient history.

The Romans introduced the forging of iron into Britain and with the use of iron tools it seems likely that the British turned to them to fashion wood for their seagoing craft. Where the Roman influence was less, particularly in Ireland, the use of hide covering persisted and there are still curraghs of this type in use off the western coast of Ireland today.

A curragh differs from a coracle in being boat-shaped and usually propelled by oars. Except for the need for greater strength, and variations to suit the shape, construction is basically the same as in a coracle. Early craft would have been made of strips of round wood. Modern frameworks are of sawn laths. Skins had to be sewn together to cover the framework. Waterproofing of joints was by natural waxes and greases, and probably not very effective so that bailing was constantly needed. Modern canvas coverings are sewn and a considerable thickness of tar, tallow and pitch mixture is built up outside.

The smallest Irish craft were of coracle form, although called curraghs, and used on the River Boyne and elsewhere for fishing until quite recently. Some seagoing curraghs were not very much bigger and intended to be paddled. Being 8ft (2.4m) to 12ft (3.6m) long they had a rounded spoon-shaped bow and a swept-up transom stern. In a Donegal paddling curragh the main strength came from a stout gunwale. Withies were bent to form the ribs of the hull and their ends taken through holes burned in the gunwale. Length-wise members were arranged fairly closely outside the ribs. In early boats they would have been lashed, but they are now nailed. The usual crew was two, with the main power provided by a man leaning over the rounded bow and using a draw-sculling action while his mate used another paddle to steer and help progress.

Modern outboard boats have not completely ousted the use of these paddling curraghs for fishing and ferrying between islands off the west Irish coast. There have been reports of cows and horses transported in them. High loads of turf (peat) were common. Some paddling curraghs also have thole pins so they can be rowed with a pair of oars like a dinghy.

Many other curraghs have been and still are built in lengths up to 30ft (9m). Construction, even at that length, was usually basically the same, without the stout central hog or keelson of most other types of boat (Plate 23). Nowadays the skin of a larger boat is made up of several thicknesses of canvas, with tar between as well as outside. A false keel and

Plate 23. A six-oared curragh, built in 1973. These boats are still in regular use in Galway Bay, Eire.

Plate 24. Interior of a modern curragh.

rubbing strips of wood may be fixed outside, but these contribute protection rather than strength.

Some Donegal boats tend to be almost parallel for most of their length, with a rather abrupt pull in to form a pointed bow, when viewed from above. In side view the bottom sweeps up towards the ends, a characteristic seen in other craft intended to be worked off beaches.

Most curraghs, like coracles, had the parts of the framework comparatively widely spaced so that the covering material was unbacked more than it was backed *(Plate 24)*. What must be a sort of transition type, although apparently dating back several centuries, is the curragh of Iniskea and Achil Island. The

ribs are covered with thin planking, fitting fairly closely, although not close enough to be watertight in itself. This takes the fabric covering and presents a smoother exterior and a more shapely hull, although some of these boats are given an angular gunwale sheer that could never be described as beautiful.

Paddles and oars must have been very rough in the early days. This was understandable, but it is surprising that users of these craft today still depend on very crude and inefficient oars and paddles, which may mean a lot of effort going to waste.

Coracle paddles tend to have long blades. In some areas it was usual to carry the coracle over one shoulder, supported by the end of the paddle pushed into a hole in the seat. In that

28

Plate 25. A Euphrates quaffah, a woven basket coated with bitumen.

case the paddle handle was straight. It was more common to have a strap on the coracle seat and carry it by that. In that case there could be some shaping to the paddle to form a hand hold, or a cross-piece was fitted like a spade handle.

In some parts of Ireland curragh oars were used through a pair of thole pins or there was a block with a hole for a single pin on the oar. The size of blade depended on the wood available, but some curraghs were rowed with blades little wider than the rest of the oars.

As with much of other Irish history it is difficult to separate fact from legend, but it does seem certain that curraghs were used for quite lengthy voyages. Celtic monks in Ireland, searching for solitude 1,200 years ago

are known to have reached Iceland in their curraghs in AD 750. As there is no prevailing wind there or back, it seems likely that they rowed both ways. They had little knowledge of navigation. They knew something about directions using the stars, but had no knowledge of latitude and longitude. In any case they did not know that Iceland was there, so they must have 'smelled' the land. Several centuries later Columbus sailed westward with a fear of falling off the edge of the flat world. Those monks were already certain that the world was round, so they did not have that fear.

St Brandon lived around AD 550. His writings about voyages are too near the truth for all of them to be ascribed to legend. The

Vikings did not get to Iceland until AD 850. The Irish monks had been there long before. St Columba travelled by curragh from Ireland and landed on Iona in AD 563. He knew nothing of what was before him and must have sensed the presence of land and used birds as guides. Many early navigators carried birds. If a bird was released and flew away, they knew that was the way towards land. Irish monks also visited Orkney and Shetland as well as the Faroes.

It is very likely that Irish monks who reached Iceland would have gone on to Greenland and then the American mainland. Norse sagas provide evidence of what could only have been settlements of Irish monks in America. The Saga of Eric the Red, who colonised Greenland, speaks of visits to the American mainland where he heard of people who wore white clothes and walked in processions carrying poles with cloths attached—a description that would fit Irish monks. The Vikings are given credit for discovering America before Columbus did, but it looks as though Irish monks in their curraghs were there a long time before them.

The coracle form of boat does not appear to have been used in many other parts of the world. Exceptions are India, with a rather similar construction to the British ones. Tibet has the ku-dru, while some in Iraq had the same shape, but the construction was very different. The craft, called a *Quaffah*, and used on the Tigris and Euphrates, was a hemispherical basket made by the coiled basketry technique, as used by many peoples for making smaller containers. Size was anything up to 10ft (3m) diameter, or more. Straw and reeds, made into a thick rope, were coiled around and the coils sewn together by wrapping with strips taken from date palm leaves, each turn being taken through the coil below *(Plate 25)*.

Stiffness was given by an inner framework of split branches fitted like ribs and tied in. The quaffah was made watertight by coating the outside of the basket with thick bitumen. Hit on the Euphrates was the favoured place for obtaining bitumen. Apparently some quaffahs were covered with leather, but this may have been as a protection against abrasion. Bitumen on the closely-woven basket was considered sufficient proofing.

A small quaffah was paddled in the same way as a British coracle. Larger ones had extra paddlers, while there are sculptures on Egyptian palace panels showing them as far back as nine centuries BC being rowed. There is a relief at the Palace of Sennacherib, of about 700 BC, showing four Assyrians on board what must have been a fairly large quaffah. Far from the Middle East, in Indo-China, almost identical craft are still used for fishing.

CHAPTER 4

North American bark and skin boats

When the white man arrived in North America he found the natives were using bark and skin boats and, to a lesser extent, dug-out craft. How long they had been doing so is not really known. The Indian's tools were of a Stone Age type and he could have been building boats in this way for a very long time, but there are no records that could produce a positive history.

The American birchbark canoe is certainly peculiar to that country, as is the kayak built by the Eskimo in the Arctic part of the continent. For modern craft the word 'canoe' may be qualified in England as a 'Canadian' canoe to distinguish it from the kayak, which is also often called a 'canoe.' While modern canoes follow a generally similar form with swept-up ends and short end decks, the original types varied considerably between different tribes and parts of the country.

Early European explorers have recorded very little detail of canoes as they first saw them, except to remark that they were light and fast and to say how many men a canoe would carry. The first known reference was by a Frenchman in 1535. Jacques Cartier reported seeing two canoes carrying a total of 17 men.

The first man to record sizes was Champlain. In 1603 near where Quebec is today he saw a canoe 8 to 9 paces long, 1½ paces wide and able to carry a pipe of wine, yet light enough to be carried by one man. Translated to modern measurements, this would be 20ft (6m) to 23ft (7m) long, 40in (1.01m) to 50in (1.37m) beam and capable of carrying about half a ton (500kg). Champlain was impressed, particularly when canoes easily passed his rowing boats. These were probably Algonkin canoes.

When Champlain attacked the Iroquois, on the lake which is now named after him, he said they had canoes about 30ft (9m) long, which were covered with oak bark (now believed to have been elm).

In 1603 Captain George Weymouth was the first Englishman to record seeing canoes, on the coast of what is now Maine. Those he saw had crews of three or four and were faster than his rowing boats. He was complimentary about the workmanship in the canoes.

Early explorers were quick to adopt canoes. In 1615 Champlain, with another Frenchman and 12 Indians, did a trip to the Great Lakes in two canoes, which he said were overcrowded. Father Jacques Marquette *(Plate 26)* and Louis Joliet made a lengthy trip in 1672 using two canoes, which must have been about 30ft (9m), to carry 30 men. By 1660 the French colonial government was issuing licences for traders to use canoes.

Indian tribes who built birchbark canoes do

Plate 26. Stamps showing a North American freight canoe of about 1672.

not appear to have built special war canoes, as happened in other parts of the world. The French seem to have had ideas about using canoes for their troops as they came nearer to building special bark war canoes than did the Indians themselves. Indians of the western side of America had built dug-out war canoes.

As canoes became adopted for trading, particularly fur trading, they became bigger and greater load carriers. However, they were still lightly-built, as portages between waterways had to be undertaken on most routes. The French actually operated a canoe factory of their own. A report of it in 1751 said they made twenty canoes per year and these were large trading canoes, about 36ft (10m) long, 5½ft (1.65m) beam and 33in (83cm) deep. Surprisingly, no other technical details have been recorded.

A bark canoe is a good example of the use of materials ready to hand. The bark favoured was from the paper birch tree, which could be peeled off, even with Stone Age tools, about ⅛in (3mm) thick. These trees grew to 100ft (30m) and large pieces of bark could be removed from their straight trunks.

Bark from spruce, elm, chestnut, basswood and cottonwood was also used, but it was birch which produced the durable craft. The roots of black spruce were used for sewing the bark together. This could be found in very long lengths no thicker than a pencil. Spruce roots were also used. White cedar grew in the same areas as birch and this was used for framing. Waterproofing of seams was done with the resin from the white or black spruce *(Plate 27)*. The work was done with stone axes and wedges, with flint knives and scrapers.

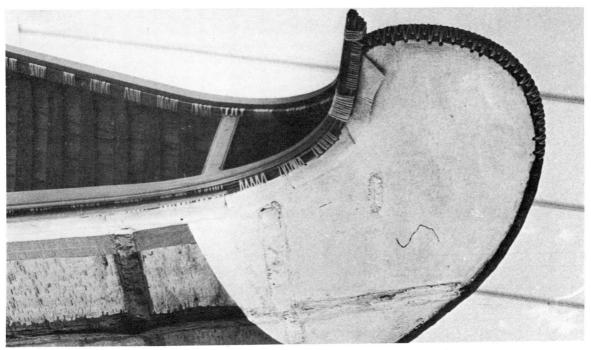

Plate 27. The end of an Ottawa bark canoe, built in 1901. The joints are proofed with spruce resin.

Bark cannot be stretched over a framework, as would be done with hide or canvas. Instead, the canoe shape was obtained in the bark and shape given by building and tensioning the framework inside afterwards. In one method of building, a framework forming what would eventually be the gunwale and thwart assembly was made first. The bark, made up into a suitable size was put on the ground under this and bent up to shape, to be held there by stakes driven in the ground. Gores were cut in the sides of the bark to allow it to shape and these were laced up. The gunwale was then raised to its correct position and internal framing added—many of the cross members merely springing lengthwise parts against the bark skin without any fixing to them.

Building a canoe required patience; partly because of the primitive tools used and partly because of the need to let soaked bark dry and set in shape. The compound curvature the bark had to take involved much slashing of gores and pulling into shape. Paddles appear to have been a matter of pride and the favoured shapes were very similar to the beaver-tail type used today.

Canoe shapes varied considerably. Some of these were due to the conditions expected to be faced, while others must have only been tribal traditions. Cross-sections were generally very stable, with a large area of near flat bottom extending for much of the length of the canoe. Ends did not sweep up much on canoes used in streams or where there was a lot of overhanging undergrowth to be passed. It

Plate 28. Freight boat in North America, circa 1860, propelled by oars.

might have been thought that low ends would have been an advantage where the canoe had to present the least windage in open water, but some tribes built their lake canoes with high ends. If the canoe had to shoot rapids, a high bow kept water out. Traders also favoured high ends when the canoe was used as a shelter. When it was turned over the ends supported it so that the centre part made a good shelter.

Because of the method of construction the bottom of a canoe might be hogged (hollow in the length) when empty, but when loaded, the light structure would give to make it slightly deeper at the centre than at the ends.

Despite their size the fur trading canoes were built in a generally similar way to the smaller craft. The canoe could be portaged by

about three men. The load was divided into lots of about 80lb (36kg), as the sort of weight a man could carry on one journey. The romantic picture of the canoe man in a trading canoe was far from true. It was back-breaking hard work.

The Indians of the north western parts of North America built birchbark canoes similar to those of the eastern part, but these were mostly family and cargo canoes. They also used birchbark to make kayak-form canoes. Although generally similar in shape to Eskimo kayaks they were made in the same way as open canoes. Some had turned-up ends, while others were little different in form from modern touring kayaks. The Indian kayak-canoe was mainly a hunting craft. Sizes were 12ft (3.65m) to 18ft (5.49m) long and 24in

(60cm) to 27in (68cm) beam. While most open canoes were symmetrical in their length, some of these kayak-canoes had their greater beam slightly aft of the centre. Both this characteristic and the sizes agree with modern thought on touring kayak design.

Of course the white man also used some of his European boatbuilding ideas and some freight craft were propelled by oars *(Plate 28)*.

The Arctic skin boats are almost exclusive to North America. Just a few are found in the Russian Arctic. The Eskimo kayak is essentially a single-seat seagoing craft intended for hunting seals. There were many variations, partly due to local preferences, but also because the Eskimo was without a plentiful supply of building material and his kayak had to be adapted to suit available driftwood and other things. Nowadays he may still build kayaks, but he is able to benefit from modern transport and get materials from elsewhere.

The Eskimo had to travel fast through the water to get close enough to throw a harpoon at a seal. This meant his kayak had to be long and narrow. The high bow lifted over ice flows. The kayak had to keep out water so the cockpit was as small as possible and the paddler wore an apron fitting tightly. He might almost be said to 'wear' his kayak. He could certainly not get in and out easily, hence the now well-known 'Eskimo roll' for righting a tipping canoe or turning a complete circle, as a survival technique. The Eskimo always used a double-bladed paddle. His harpoon and line were on the deck and the seal, if caught, went on a platform behind the paddler.

The quality of construction varied. Greenland and Alaskan kayaks were examples of good craftsmanship *(Plate 29)*.

Copies of kayaks used by sea canoeists in Europe are mostly based on the Greenland design.

The usual cross-section shows as stable a form as is possible with the narrow beam. Most kayaks had a multi-chine section, but others had V or flat bottoms.

A kayak is built of a number of lengthwise members held into shape by cross frames, with the main strength provided by gunwale members and possibly another stout piece along the keel line. A framework was built completely and the skin stretched over it, in contrast to the birchbark canoe where the framework was tensioned into the skin.

The covering had to be available skins, but the Alaskans preferred the bearded seal, while the Aleuts favoured the sea lion. Caribou skins have been used. Hides were left to 'sweat,' then scraped clean and dried until needed. They were sewn together to make up a skin, then soaked and stretched over the framework.

The umiak was the Eskimo's freight and family boat, for transport of goods and people. The general form was not unlike a dory, with a flattish narrow bottom and well-flared sides, but the framework was built up like a kayak hull, then a skin of walrus hide stretched over it. Tensioning was by hide thongs from holes in the skin over the gunwales. The whole boat was quite light, so could be manhandled ashore when necessary. The method of construction gave great flexibility, both to the framework and to the skin. Floating ice was a hazard, but the sprung skin and the flexing of the framework allowed a considerable amount of distortion on impact, where a more rigid skin might have been pierced.

A umiak might be 35ft (10m) long, and was

usually paddled. The Eskimo did not favour rowing, but he has now adapted to the outboard motor.

It is believed that the Plains Indians of the central part of North America built craft very similar to the British coracle. They avoided joints in the hides used as skins of these 'bull boats,' so quite often they were too small to carry a paddler. Instead they were loaded with a cargo and towed by a swimmer.

Both the canoe and the kayak have developed into popular craft today. Modern factory-produced canoes are available in several sizes. What is wrongly thought of in Europe as a traditional American canoe is a beautiful carvel-built wooden craft, but this is a product of modern craftsmanship *(Plate 30)*. Another type has reasonably close-fitting planks, but is covered by painted canvas. Mass-produced aluminium canoes stand up to rough use and many are now manufactured in glassfibre. Canoes have been used competitively in canoe slalom, but the craft developed for this have now become almost kayak-shape and the only difference is that the canoeist(s) kneels and uses a single-bladed paddle. Sprint racing canoes have little in common with traditional shapes, but the form is low and long, with the paddler on one knee using a long spadelike paddle.

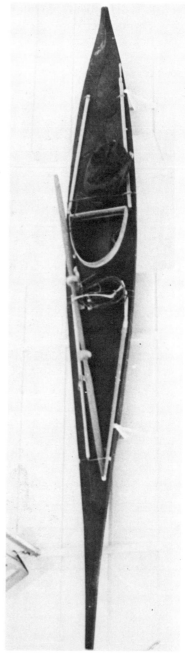

Plate 29. Eskimo kayak, from Baffin Land, covered with seal-skin.

36

Plate 30. British river canoes, used for hire. The canoe in the foreground is carvel built, while the others are clinker built.

CHAPTER 5

Mediterranean craft

The Egyptian practices of recording things on tombs and palaces and of burying belongings with dead kings have given us evidence of boats in use many centuries BC. A representation of a vessel with many oarsmen may still be found on a wall of the temple of Deir el Bahri, near Thebes. This was a ship of Queen Hatshepsut and the carving was done at least 3,500 years ago. Size was about 70ft (21m) long and 18ft (5.5m) beam. The Egyptians were not seamen and most of their boats were used on the River Nile, which was very much the centre of their life. Its waters were certainly their lifeline, as the success of crops depended on irrigation from the river and much transport of goods took place via the river. From what is known of Egyptian boats, most of them would not have been strong enough to stand up to use at sea, although some appear to have coasted inshore to the 'Land of Punt,' probably Somaliland.

An actual ship, dismantled and buried with King Khufa at Giza 4,500 years ago has been recovered. This was 152ft (46m) long and joints were made with dowels and copper staples. It has been re-assembled and preserved so as to stand beside Khufu's Great Pyramid.

Egypt is not a country of forests. There are few timber trees of any great size. Palms do not produce wood which is suitable for boat building. Consequently timber was very scarce in Egypt. This meant that boats had to be built with short lengths of any available wood. The method of construction involved sewing and lashing wood together, to make up the length and to produce the correct cross-section. Egyptian craft were without a stout lengthwise member, such as a hog or keel, to provide strength and rigidity. The boats had no timbers or frames, in the modern sense. Because of this method of building a shell without much supporting framework, an Egyptian hull was weak and easily distorted.

Such a boat might sag at the ends and become hollow in the length if nothing was done about it. The Egyptians held up the ends and prevented this by trussing the boat, with two or more posts and cables tensioned over them from end to end—rather like repairing the damage before it happened, instead of building the hull so that it could not happen. Within living memory a similar idea was used to strengthen the necessarily shallow Mississippi River Boats.

Acacia wood was commonly used. Joints in adjoining planks were staggered and some end to end joints appear to have been of dovetail form. Planks had to be made up from pieces as short as 3ft (1m). Herodotus likened their building with short pieces to bricklaying. As the unframed hull was weak and flexible so that any caulking might work out, boats were often tied around with cables outside, to keep the planks pulled together. Tomb drawings show that Egyptian craftsmen had tools like adzes and chisels.

This practise carried over into the early centuries AD. When St Paul was being taken by sea to Rome, in the events leading up to the wrecking on Malta in AD 62 we read in the Bible in Acts 27 how the sailors used tackle to undergird the ship, meaning they tightened ropes around it to stop planks springing apart. This was no small boat. Although we are not given its size, it was big enough to carry 276 people.

Egyptian craft had sail as well as oars, but little was known of the art of sailing, except as a means of making progess when the wind was blowing the same way as the boat was intended to go. As the wind was usually north and against the current on the River Nile, this was made good use of, but at other times the boats were rowed; probably by slaves.

Seagoing craft developed in the Eastern Mediterranean, which was then known as the Middle Sea. Around the Mediterranean many civilizations rose and fell. There were many island and mainland empires and states. Some states whose names have come down through history were little more than towns. For instance, the Phoenicians came from a small city/state on the shore of what is now Lebanon. They ventured past the Pillars of Hercules (Gibraltar), but most of the early seafarers would not go out of the Mediterranean.

The Phoenicians were the sailor adventurers of the Middle Sea. They built sturdy ships from the timber of Tyre and Sidon. They are known to have voyaged to Greece, Italy, North Africa and Spain. They founded Carthage and Cadiz. They reached Britain to trade for tin. About 600 BC there is fairly well authenticated evidence that they circumnavigated Africa from east to west. Herodotus describes how they went ashore in the autumn, sowed corn, waited until it could be reaped and continued their voyage. Modern knowledge of these waters show that such a trip could be possible with oars and sail, using monsoons down the east coast and around the Cape of Good Hope and trade winds up the west coast.

Phoenician craft were long and narrow. Their prows were often given a horse head. In the Bible, in the 27th chapter of Ezekiel we read of their ships:

'They have taken cedars from Lebanon to make masts for thee. Of the oaks of Bashan have they made thine oars.'

The Romans dominated all of the land around the Mediterranean for a long time, but they were always soldiers rather than seafarers. Before they came to power the eastern half of the Mediterranean was dominated by the Greeks. Before them the Mycenaeans and Minoans from Crete were known to have built seagoing craft.

Although the Egyptians had fighting ships, these were mainly for use on the river. Crete is believed to have had the first real navy. This was about 4,000 years ago. They built galleys, which appear to have been constructed something like the Egyptian craft, but with more internal framing so that the whole structure was more rigid. Construction was light as propulsion was mainly by oars.

The word 'galley' is often automatically associated with 'slave,' but in the Cretan galleys the oarsmen were free men and this was considered an honourable trade. A description of one galley gives its dimensions as about 60ft (18m) by 10ft (3m). It had a tall false prow on it with the carved head of a sacred bull. On the stern post was the Cretan royal double axe symbol.

All boats in those days had pointed sterns. This galley had a decked-over bow big enough to hold 15 fighting men, who wore leather armour and carried bronze axes and spears. There was a similar and smaller poop deck aft, for more fighting men, and two steersmen, with steering sweeps each side of the stern post. There was a central mast, to take a square sail for use in a following wind, but this was not trusted and the real power came from the oarsmen.

This boat had eleven oars on each side and each was pulled by a single oarsman. Time was kept by a rowing master sitting below the poop. He shouted and used a wooden whistle. The master of the ship was above him on the poop deck and called down orders, in the same way as messages are now passed from the bridge to the engine room. The galley could be manoeuvred by the oars and it would have been got under way by several short choppy strokes, and these then lengthened, as oarsmen start rowing craft today.

When the Cretan civilization was at its peak, the Greeks were still barbarians. As the Cretan zenith passed, the Greek civilization rose and they began to build seagoing ships bigger than the Cretan ones. While the Greeks never found a good way of holding a ship together, their craft were much better designed than those which had gone before, possibly encouraged by the fact that wood was not as scarce and could be obtained in long pieces.

The Greeks have recorded their sailor heroes and nautical exploits, probably as a mixture of fantasy and fact. There may have been errors in translation. Homer tells how Odysseus built a boat, after felling twenty trees with a bronze axe. Calypso brought him augers so that he could bore each piece and join the parts with trenails and dowels. The translator said he fitted a rudder, but this was more likely to have been a steering oar. A rudder, as we understand the word today, did not come until some time later.

A Greek ship of about 500 BC is described as being 130ft (40m) long and 16ft (5m) beam. It had a keel and a false oak keel outside for beaching. There were ribs and lengthwise strips for stiffening. The skin was 3in (7.5cm) fir planking, held to the framing with wood dowels and bronze nails and caulked with pitch and tow. For the size of the ship this was a rather thin skin, but the boat was designed as a massive frame to support a ram, while being as light as possible for rowing. The ship itself was a weapon, with a triple bronze spike extending from the prow. Above this was a shorter rounded ram, called a proembolion. Besides giving a smashing blow, this also helped in disengaging, as the ship would be in difficulty if it could not be released from a sinking opponent.

With the oarsmen pulling at full strength a ramming speed of 10 knots was possible for a short burst. The full crew was about 200 men and the ship could only remain at sea for a few days without the need to replenish food and water.

The Greek fighting ships were long and narrow and propelled mainly by oars. Their cargo boats depended mainly on sail and could only be manoeuvred in harbour with oars.

Roman power grew as Greek power diminished, but Roman galleys showed little improvement on the Greek ones. The

Phoenicians are credited with the invention of the bireme—a ship with one bank of oars above another on each side. The Phoenicians had learned the value of a keel as a strength member, but they could not build long narrow boats sufficiently strong that they would not break in two when supported unevenly on waves. The extra rows of oarsmen were a way of getting extra power without lengthening the ship. The name quinquereme they also used probably meant a larger number of oars rather than even more banks of oars. The Romans developed the trieme, with three banks of oars at each side. Timekeeping was by a man called a hortator beating a drum.

The Romans devised the forerunner of the outrigger for rowing. This was an apostis, a sort of gallery outside the hull supporting the oar fulcrums, so as to increase leverage and allow more room inside the hull, or a narrower and faster hull for the same length of oars.

After the power of Rome lessened, the leaders in shipping were then around Constantinople. Most of the north side of the Mediterranean was Christian, while most of the south side was Moslem. When they were not fighting each other they preyed on their neighbours' shipping. This was coming up to the Middle Ages, when the thoughts of Northern European nations were turning to sail, but the mainly small Mediterranean states maintained fleets of galleys, which were much the same as in the heyday of the Greeks and Romans. A description of one galley about 120ft (37m) long gives the number of oarsmen as 144, plus about 50 soldiers, sailors and officers.

Some galleys became excessively large and were called galleass. One is described as carrying 1,020 men, of which 468 were oarsmen, pulling 52 oars, each about 48ft (14.5m) long and worked by nine men.

Such a large craft was found impracticable. It was described as very beautiful at a distance, but you did not get close or downwind because of the stench. The slaves were the engines of the ship, chained to their oars, tormented and living in their own filth. They were fed for the same reason that fuel is fed to an engine, but they were not fed much or often and the difference was made up with a whip.

The life of a slave in a galley of AD 1550 has been recorded by one of them who escaped. There were four slaves to each of 38 oars. When not rowing, the oars were drawn in over the slaves' knees. The oar ports were 4ft (1.2m) above the water. The deck was not far above the head of the sitting slave. His chains would not allow standing, in any case. The slaves held the oar by a handle, called a manette. To make a stroke the slaves got on to their feet and pushed the oar forward and downward to clear the water. Then they pulled upwards and backwards as far as they could reach to pull the blade through the water. The man furthest inboard would have to go further forward and extend further backwards than his mates

In 1571 there was the last great battle dominated by galleys, when a fleet of Christian allies crushed the Turks at the Battle of Lepanto. By then sailing ships were large and stoutly built, so that rams had no effect on them. Cannons had come into use so it was possible to blow a hole in a lightly-planked galley without actually bringing the boat into contact with it. France kept galleys as prison hulks until the Revolution at the end of the eighteenth century. Spain kept some into the nineteenth century. Oarsmen

Plate 31. Typical Mediterranean carvel built craft, from Turkey.

Plate 32. The windlass used to haul Turkish craft ashore.

Plate 33. A Maltese Luzzu.

had been used in battle for 6,000 years, but their days had ended.

Although some Mediterranean boats were clinker-built, the vast majority were, and still are, planked flush, in what is now usually called carvel-planking *(Plate 31)*. Today the Greek boats still show a feeling for line and are graceful shapes. Some of the best boat building is found in Turkey. This is supposed to date from the days of the Ottoman empire when the Sultans spared no expense to import the best craftsmen to build their galleys. There boats were hauled up on the beaches *(Plate 32)*.

Small craft of the Mediterranean were characterised by considerable sheer to the gunwale, with the upswept end finishing in high prows and stern posts *(Plate 33)*. This is seen today in many small craft around the Mediterranean. There may be some carry-over from the days of the decorative ends and the rams of galleys, but there is no real justification today for these features. In Malta the dghaisa is an all-purpose harbour boat propelled by oars, with the oarsman usually standing and facing forward *(Plate 34)*. The looms of the oars are long enough for him to need to cross his hands when they pass. This boat has very high decorative ends *(Plate 35)*.

The high ends are retained even in the large inter-island Gozo boat, or dghaisa-tal-pass, which carries sail and the rudder head has to be brought high for the tiller to clear the stern post decorative extension. Also of note is the

43

Plate 34. A Maltese oarsman faces forward as he rows to his dghaisa.

Plate 35. The decorative end of a Maltese dghaisa.

Plate 36. A Maltese fishing boat.

Kajjik, the Maltese work-boat, built like a cut off dghaisa, with a transom stern *(Plate 36)*.

A good sheer and high ends make launching and returning through surf easier. These conditions are not typical of the Mediterranean, yet many craft have very high ends. One very special high-ended craft is the Venetian gondola *(Plate 37)*.

In the thirteenth century the name 'gondola' was given to a small fighting galley, intended for ramming. The name then went to a small coastal boat and to a double-ended canal boat, before settling on the Venetian craft of the present day. While the majority of these craft are now used for pleasure, it was the general-purpose transport of Venice.

The visitor to Venice today sees gondolas which are very little different from those of 500 years ago. The hull is light and rather canoelike. It can be between 30ft (9m) and 50ft (15m) long, but most today are about 36ft (11m) long. Beam is about 4ft (1.2m) and the draught is very slight.

The hull is always painted black. This was a law of the Doge Barbarigo at the end of the fifteenth century and is still enforced. Construction is of quite thin planking over about 40 light frames. The hull may be open for much of its length, then the ends are decked and there may be a canopy for goods or passengers arranged centrally. At the bow there is a raised decorative pattern, believed to be a carry-over from the ram of the galley. The stern also has a raised graceful projection.

Plate 37. The Venetian Gondola.

The ends of the hull rise above the water, so that a rather short part of the boat is in the water and it can turn easily. The oarsman always stands on the port side of his platform at the stern and uses his single oar in a raised carved walnut 'forcola' on the starboard side. While he is adept at both rowing and steering with this oar, the hull is designed to help counteract the turning effect this lopsided push is bound to have. The gondola is curved in its length in plan view, with the starboard side 8in (20cm) shorter than the port side to provide an automatic correction to the thrust of the oar *(Plate 38)*.

There were supposed to be as many as 10,000 gondolas in use, some centuries ago. In the mid-nineteenth century there were 2,000 in use. The building of more bridges and the competition of power boats has reduced the numbers to a few hundred. All gondolas in use

now are old. The art of building them is dying as few new craftsmen are being trained.

Smaller rowing craft from all around the Mediterranean have family likenesses. Nearly all boats are double-ended, with a pointed stern very little fuller than the bow. The high ends, reaching above the essential end posts are usual, as already mentioned. It is unusual to find a local transom-sterned rowing boat in the Mediterranean. Hulls have always been flush planked. In other parts of the world carvel planking has not been regarded as satisfactory except in craft large enough to justify planks ¾in (2cm) thick, because of the difficulty of caulking anything thinner. Many Mediterranean boats have had planks only half this thickness.

Frames have always been sawn to shape and built on to quite a heavy keel, instead of the lighter bent frames or timbers of Northern

Plate 38. In this view of a gondola, the twisted shape is easily seen.

European small craft. Stiffness in many small Mediterranean boats is still by a sunk deck. This has end and side decks at thwart level, with a stout stiffener outside, which also acts as a rubber to protect the hull. Scuppers may be cut above this to allow water to run out from the sunk deck.

This type of craft can be seen used off the beaches of the South of France and Spain, as well as in Italy and further east. The modern French version is called a 'pointu.' The design has evolved over thousands of years. In the last century some of the emigrants from Mediterranean countries have taken the idea with them and the influence of these Middle Sea designs can be seen in local boats of the USA and elsewhere.

CHAPTER 6

Viking craft

The design of European boats away from the Mediterranean influence has been dominated by the craft of the Norsemen or Vikings. Theirs were the first craft to be rowed and sailed about the northern seas. Other countries had their skin boats and other primitive craft on inland waters, but these were the first real seagoing boats. Other countries could do no better than follow the Norse designs. In fact, with all the modern knowledge of naval architecture available it is difficult to do more than improve in detail on these craft, when considering their design in relation to the purposes for which they were built.

These Scandinavian seamen came from Norway, Sweden and Denmark. In old Norse *Vik* means 'fjord,' or inlet, while *ing* means 'son of,' so a Viking was a son of the fjord. The coast of Norway, in particular, is harsh and cut with many inlets. For much of it the only means of transport was by sea. This was an unproductive land. The sea offered the only outlet for anyone with ambition. It was natural that the unoccupied male population should consider forays against the farmlands of England and other countries.

These were the Dark Ages—those centuries about which not so much is known in detail. The Vikings' activities ranged through many centuries up to about the eleventh.

Christianity had not reached the Norsemen. They believed in their gods Odin and Thor. Their warlike beliefs and blind faith probably led them on to succeed in what must have been very hazardous voyages.

In the Viking faith physical courage was the highest virtue and death in battle was a sure way to heaven. They believed that valkyries, maidens sent by the god Odin, selected the warriors to be killed in battle and escorted to Valhalla (heaven).

A contemporary writer describes them as an energetic, turbulent, warlike people with a talent for making trouble. They certainly made plenty of trouble for people who lived on the coast and up rivers that the Norsemen's longships could navigate.

Although the Norsemen were not given to carving pictures of their boats on tombs as were the Egyptians, they shared with them the practice of burying boats with their dead chieftains. Two very fine specimens have been unearthed from grave mounds at the Gokstad and Oseberg farms in Norway. These date from the ninth century. A much earlier boat, called the Nydam boat, was dug from a bog in Jutland. It is now in a museum at Schleswig, Germany. This was 76ft (23m) long and 11ft (3.35m) beam, and was built in the fourth century. This ship has holes which make it appear that she was scuttled—probably her

Plate 39. A one-third scale model of a Viking ship.

Plate 40. A drawing of a Viking longship showing pole mast.

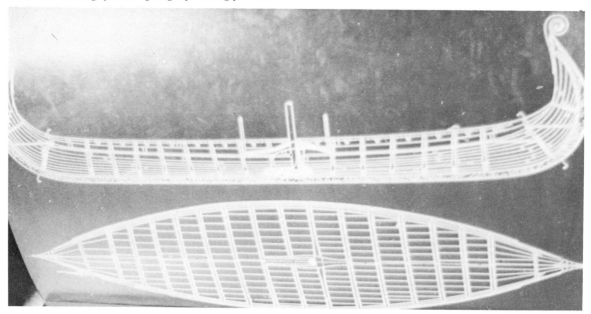

crew sank her rather than let her be captured.

The Oseberg ship owes its preservation to blue clay. It was dug up in 1904. This was 70ft (21m) long and used 15 pairs of oars. From its build this was considered to have been a pleasure craft. The Gokstad ship, excavated in 1888, was similar in size to the Nydam boat, although 500 years more recent.

Viking ships were built in a similar way to the clinker craft of today, with a substantial hog/keel member providing strength. The centre section was of broad flattish stable form, and there was considerable sheer to the gunwale line, sweeping up to high ends *(Plate 39)*. Overall lines were generally similar to Mediterranean craft of similar size and purpose. Like them, they always had pointed sterns.

Viking longboats were comparatively shallow. Oars were used over the gunwales more often than through holes in the sides. They were only single-banked and with one man per oar. The Viking fighting men were also the oarsmen. There were never slaves nor a trade of oarsman separate from the soldier.

The clinker planks were adzed to shape from logs. Projections, or cleats, were left at intervals on the inside. These were used for lashings to light ribs sprung in after the ship was planked. The overlapping planks were caulked and joined with nails and pegs. A Viking boatbuilder seeing a modern Scandinavian boatbuilder at work would understand what was going on, and even be able to help.

Figureheads were used to frighten evil spirits, but these were made removable so that they could be taken in when close to shore, and friendly land spirits would not be frightened. Alternatively they might represent a dragon or fearsome sea monster, which no doubt frightened the peaceful people the Vikings raided.

A Viking ship had a single pole mast near the centre *(Plate 40)* and a square sail hung from a yard. No doubt the high winds of northern waters could be used and the Norsemen knew something of close-hauled sailing by bringing the yard nearer fore-and-aft, but as their craft were very shallow draught they must have made considerable leeway. With their low freeboard they could not safely heel much and would swamp easily. This, coupled with inevitable leaks, must have made constant baling necessary.

Steering a Viking ship was by a single large blade at the stern and always on the right side *(Plate 41)*. This was the 'stjornbord' or 'steering board'—and 1,000 years later 'starboard' is still the name of that side of the ship.

The oarsmen had benches or thwarts. Each warrior hung his shield over the side of the ship. Stores went under the benches. An oarsman would stand to get more power. Timekeeping was by singing songs with endless verses—probably an explanation of the lengthy Norse sagas.

As happened elsewhere, Viking ships became bigger over the years. Early craft were entirely open. Then came a shelter tent forward for those resting. Later larger craft had some decking, with living space and protected storage space. Many were around the size of the excavated boats already described. A 'skuta' was said to be 80ft (24m) long and have 30 oars. The 'ask' and the 'skeid' had as many as 64 oars and could carry a crew of 200 men.

Whatever their size, Viking longboats must have been cold and wet craft to use in the

Plate 41. Starboard side steering oar on a longship.

attacked. In AD 844 they had ranged as far south as Lisbon and Cadiz to attack them. The Vikings cruised up rivers and attacked both Hamburg and Paris in AD 845. In AD 860 they went into the Mediterranean as far as Pisa, in what is now Italy. They made inland voyages from the Baltic along the Volga as far as the Caspian Sea and via the Dnieper as far as the Black Sea.

These last voyages were made by Vikings from Sweden, who were less warlike and more intent on trading. They were called Varangians. They rowed their longships thousands of miles. One Varangian, called Rurik, is said to have founded Novgorod on the Volga in AD 862. Those who got through to the Black Sea are said to have founded the fair-haired bodyguard to the Byzantine emperor, the Varangian Guard.

The Vikings had roamed the northern waters. They had rounded the North Cape and penetrated to the White Sea. The Orkney and Shetland Islands were then Norse rather than British. They had rounded Scotland and actually settled in Ireland, where Dublin is now. Their longships had reached Iceland in AD 874.

In AD 986 Bjarni Herjulfson went off course when voyaging from Iceland to Greenland. He continued and sighted what must have been the mainland of America. Leif Ericson then used Bjarni's boat, went to Greenland and sailed in search of the land that had been sighted. He found a wild rocky shore and landed at what he called 'Vinland' (wineland), where grapes grew in profusion. As a result of his discovery Thorfinn Karksefni took 160 people and settled for several years on the mainland. While there his wife bore him a son—the first child of European parentage to be born in America.

northern waters. Their tough crews made voyages which would be considered good in modern craft of their size.

Most recorded voyages took place in the ninth century AD. Forays against the British Isles had been frequent. Northern parts of Scotland are nearer to Scandinavia than to the south of England. In AD 843 Nantes was

HIC EXEVNT:CABALLI DE NAVIBVS · ET HIC:MILITES

Plate 42. *The Normans land at Pevensey with their horses*

After withstanding harassment from Indians for a long time, this party finally gave up and rowed and sailed their longboats back to Iceland.

The Vikings settled on many coastal parts of Europe. One of these areas was Normandy—a name coming from Norsemen. Normandy had been colonized and the people had settled peacefully, then their Duke William prepared to invade Britain. These Viking colonists had not lost their skill at building longboats. There is no record of the total built and used, but in one amphibious operation 7,000 men and 3,000 horses were transported at night across the Channel. The ships were built in the Viking tradition, mostly at the mouth of the River Dives on the Normandy coast. They were given dragon

heads and shields were hung outboard in the true Viking manner. Most of the boats were fitted with 32 oars. William waited for a favourable wind so that his oarsmen would not be too tired when they got there. They were not, and every schoolboy knows that William the Conqueror defeated Harold at the Battle of Hastings in AD 1066.

The history of this event is pictorially recorded in the Bayeux Tapestry. This is a fantastic linen tapestry 231ft (70m) long and 20in (51cm) wide, that was hand woven at the bidding of William's wife, Matilda. The tapestry can still be seen at Bayeux in the French province of Normandy.

Parts of the tapestry show the crowded longboats crossing the Channel and landing at Hastings. William's flagship *Mora* is shown

53

with a masthead lantern topped by a cross blessed by the Pope. William is supposed to have tripped and fell on to his hands as he stepped ashore. As he recovered, clutching sand and soil, he is supposed to have said, 'I have taken England with both my hands.' Whatever else he had done, he was to unify the many factions in England and make her into a single very sea-conscious people *(Plate 42)*.

Replicas of Viking ships are still built and used for youth training and other purposes, but a replica that attempted to reproduce an earlier voyage was built in 1893 and sailed across the Atlantic. As near as possible this was a reproduction of the Gokstad ship. Captain Magnus Anderson took her from Bergen to St Johns, Newfoundland, without the calls for rest at Iceland and Greenland that the original Vikings must have had. The crossing was made without escort or help in 27 days. This longboat was taken to the Chicago World's Fair. She may still be seen in Chicago's Lincoln Park. There would not have been much rowing on that crossing. The captain reported that the hull was very flexible and the whole hull worked in storms, but she stayed remarkably tight. This trip proved the feasibility of the earlier voyages and proved the sea-keeping qualities of these boats.

CHAPTER 7

Northern European boats

The majority of boats used in the last few centuries in and around the countries of Northern Europe have shown a Viking influence. Of course, many British and other fighting craft at the time of Viking activities and until after the Norman invasion would have been copies of the Norse craft. After 1066 any local British and Viking types would have been integrated. Around the British Isles until recent days, clinker planking (sometimes called 'clincher,' 'clench' or 'lapstrake') on sawn and bent frames, with fairly substantial keel members, has been the common method of construction for work and pleasure boats for many centuries. The major difference from Viking craft has been in the fitting of a transom.

It is the underwater shape of a boat that matters most. For rowing or sailing with the minimum effort and the best performance the underwater lines should allow the water to pass astern with little disturbance. This can be achieved by making the boat double-ended, with pointed stern as well as bow. The pointed stern also has some advantage in parting and riding over waves coming from astern. This is an advantage in coping with a following sea and when taking a boat through surf. The Vikings needed these qualities.

However, for load carrying, the pointed stern represents a lot of length without much capacity. When a boat is rowed, any cargo or passengers are likely to be aft. With a pointed stern, this load has to be some way forward of the stern post, so that the boat trims properly. A transom cuts off and fills out the hull at this point. Providing the hull is shaped so that all, or nearly all, of the transom is above the normal waterline, the underwater lines can still give a reasonably smooth run to the water, while there is plenty of capacity and buoyancy where the greatest load will have to come. Because of this, many craft intended for harbours and inland waters, which might be used for coastal work without the need to be launched through surf, were given transom sterns. A transom stern is also an advantage when working fishing lines or nets *(Plates 43 and 44)*.

On London River (the Thames tideway) rowing boats had considerable use as transports for passengers and goods in the Middle Ages and right up to the coming of reasonable and clean roads in the nineteenth century. Travelling by water must have been preferable to moving about the city by land. The general-purpose craft were wherries (possibly a corruption of 'ferries'). The trade of Thames waterman was an honourable one. A typical Thames wherry was quite long and with a high pointed bow, ending in a sharp iron nose. It was beamy and of stable section,

Plate 43. Picardy fishing boat, used for stern fishing.

Plate 44. A craft similar to the Picardy boat. The sloping transom gives extra buoyancy when shortening nets.

pulled, usually, by one man with a pair of oars used through cut-out rowlocks in the sides or with thole pins. The watermen in their wherries served shipping and other craft, but they were, in some ways, the taxis of those days, and could be hailed from steps for passage to other steps.

A general-purpose and fishing boat on the Thames was called a peter boat, the name coming from St Peter, the patron saint of fishermen. These boats were used on the fresh water part of the river as well as the tidal reaches, but those on the non-tidal were smaller. The peter boat was fairly full-sectioned and double-ended, with the stern more rounded and bluff than the bow. There was decking at thwart level, both at the ends and the sides, showing a Norwegian origin. These craft were used to fish for smelt, lamprey and several other fish. A fish well may have been built in. Construction was clinker and heavy, but although up to 25ft (7.5m) long they were normally handled by one man with a pair of oars. The last of these boats were found between Hammersmith and Richmond.

The method of fishing was called 'hebbing' (possibly more correctly 'ebbing'). The men concerned were called 'hebbermen' and they put a netlike 'hebbing weir' across the stream to stop and catch the fish. Pollution of the river by sewages directly emptied in stopped fish coming up as far from the sea, and hebbing had to cease.

It is only in recent years that pollution control has made it possible for sea fish to penetrate the waters upriver of London.

Another boat peculiar to the Thames was the randan, used by three oarsmen and a cox. The centre man pulled a pair of oars (sculls), while the men in front and behind him used one oar only each. The name 'randan' was first applied to the method of rowing, but then passed to the boat. This arrangement gives a certain versatility to the arrangement, particularly when one or more of the crew had to cease rowing and attend to other things. Randans were used by some Thames watermen as well as the Custom House and the Thames Conservancy. Working boats of this type were used on the tidal Thames between Teddington locks and Gravesend. A later and lighter version was used on the upper Thames as an alternative to a skiff.

Boat names were not always consistent. In the days when few people travelled far it did not matter if the name in one locality was different from that in another so long as everyone in one place knew what was meant. Even today, what is a 'dinghy' to most people becomes a 'punt' at some southern British ports (Plate 45). The word 'skiff' is now used for a lightly-built pleasure rowing boat, usually with one or two pairs of sculls, possibly with outriggers or a hull broad at the gunwales to keep the rowlocks well out (Plates 46 and 47). This has been the generally accepted name, particularly on the upper Thames and other non-tidal placid rivers.

Heavier boats were once called 'gigs.' These were used on tidal waters, but in some places they were called 'skiffs.' The word 'skiff' was, and still may be, used for an open rowing and sailing boat used for oyster fishing, even when it was quite large.

Wherries, peter boats and other craft were extremely heavily built, which may have been necessary to stand up to hard work, but they must have been difficult to row, particularly against a tide. As boatbuilding skill progressed, lighter working boats came into use in the latter half of the nineteenth century, generally described as 'watermen's skiffs.'

Plate 45. Punts can be paddled as well as poled, when the water is too deep for poling.

Plate 46. A light skiff of the Victorian era. Construction is of mahogany.

Plate 47. Double sculling skiff, with gunwale rowlocks.

Plate 48. Forward part of a Thames Watermans' skiff, built in Gravesend in 1873. The boards under the thwarts kept the seats dry when not in use.

Hulls were deep and roomy, but comparatively lightly built, with clinker planking on sawn frames. There was a certain amount of decoration, but the accent was on utility *(Plate 48).*

Such a skiff was normally rowed and handled by one man, who might sometimes take an apprentice to pull a second pair of oars. It might carry as many as eight passengers or up to two tons of merchandise, in its ferrying trips between parts of the shore or between shore and ship.

These skiffs were used for early professional racing (see Chapter 11), and could be arranged for four oarsmen. Oars were used through thole pins, but these were shaped with wedge-shaped projections, as are still found on some pleasure skiffs, instead of the round pins more common on other craft.

Very heavy workboats, more like small barges, were used in many parts of Britain. The Fenland punt *(Plate 49)* is an example, used for carrying cargo and eel fishing. It was given a hollowed slightly rockered bottom, to prevent it sticking to mud. The cog was similar. One of these, probably dating from the thirteenth century was found in the bed of the River Rother in 1824. Similar craft were in use on the River Parrett in Somerset until early in the twentieth century.

When a boat has to be launched off and return to a shallow beach, it has to keep its bow to the sea, leaving bow first, but returning stern first. To cope with these conditions boats

Plate 49. A Fenland punt, used for cargo work and eel fishing. Propelled by quanting.

have been devised with fairly deep forefoots, yet extremely shallow sterns. Typical is the coble. These are often referred to as 'Yorkshire cobles,' but the type spread along the north-east coast of Northumberland and over the Scottish border. Cobles were used for fishing and carried sail as well as being rowed. The type has not died out, but most modern cobles have engines.

A writer during the period of the last century, before the days of mechanical power, described a coble:

'The bows are very sharp and very high, with a great sheer to throw off the sea, and depth to give lateral resistance. The sharp bows fall away rapidly, until all the aft portion of the boat is quite flat and shallow.

The keel, which commences with the bow, ends amidships, and from there to the stern are two keels, or draughts, one each side of the flat bottom. The stern is very raking and the rudder projects a considerable distance below it. Thus the whole lateral resistance of the boat is given by the deep rudder and the deep bow. These boats are very sensitive to any touch of the helm; they will go wonderfully close to the wind and at a perfectly marvellous speed; their sharp, flaring bows throw off any reasonable sea, and altogether they are admirably suited to the work which they have to undergo. Then, when they have to be beached, their bows are turned to the sea, the rudder is unshipped and the boat backed ashore

Plate 50. Stern of a Yorkshire coble showing plank-like rudder, lifted when the boat was brought stern first to the beach.

under oars, where she sits high and dry, as far as her stern is concerned.'

Cobles have not changed much and that reads as a fair testimonial to the seamen who designed and evolved the coble.

A coble was 25ft (7.5m)-30ft (9m) long. Its hull was stoutly planked with wide boards laid clinker fashion. A Yorkshire coble had some tumblehome, with the top plank each side sloping inwards. A Scottish skiff, of basically similar design and purpose, was without the tumblehome and may have had a continuous external keel, instead of the change from keel to a flat 'ram plank' from the centre of the boat to the stern.

Although most cobles had flat raking transom sterns, some were taken to a point and were called 'mules.'

The long deep rudder was little more than a plank, in shape *(Plate 50),* and projected some way below the hull, so it could not be shipped until the boat had been rowed through the surf into deeper water and it had to be removed some way out when returning. This meant that the oarsmen had to keep the bow towards the sea and avoid broaching while backing their coble on to the beach.

Of course, boat design in the Scandinavian countries did not stop with the Vikings. The deeply indented coastline of Norway and the considerable amount of water in and around Sweden and Finland, have made boats a way of life. Most smaller Scandinavian wooden craft still show the Viking influence, more than do the wooden boats of other European countries. Clinker boats of Britain, France and the Low Countries tend to have fairly large numbers of comparatively narrow planks. Scandinavian boats have rather fewer planks each side. Narrow planks allow a more rounded shape, but involve a lot of work in building. Wide planks, possibly as few as four per side, give a multi-chine section rather than a rounded one. Wider planks also have to be thicker to give enough strength the short way of the grain.

Frames of these boats tended to be few compared with boats of other countries and often sawn to shape, where other countries favoured bent frames. Nearly all of these boats were double-ended, with fuller sterns than bows. The general appearance was much the same as the Thames peter boat, and they are obviously related. Traditionally, there were seven oak planks each side.

Boats of this type are still used off Danish islands and the beaches of Jutland. The smaller ones, 12ft (3.6m)-16ft (4.9m), are rowed, while larger craft are powered. They are used as pleasure boats, but earlier ones were used for fishing. The boats are heavily constructed to withstand daily beaching. Launching and recovery is by winch and cable. The boats are hauled up the beach and launching is by an outhaul through a block on a buoy.

In some parts of the world the word 'skiff' implies a flat-bottomed craft with planked sides. There have been Norwegian skiffs, which were double-ended small, but not light, rowing boats. The stem and stern posts curved down to a bottom which broadened to form a flat base. The sides had considerable flare and were made up by three broad planks arranged clinker fashion and with only a small number of frames. Thwarts helped to provide stiffness and the boat would be rowed by one or two oarsmen. The frames towards the ends were canted inwards so as to follow the shape of the planking better (the top of the frame nearer the centre of the boat length than the bottom). Natural crooks might

Plate 51. A Somerset peat boat. Propelled by pole, it is similar to a dory and shows Scandinavian influence.

Plate 52. A clinker built pram dinghy.

be used. One of the crooks excavated from an eleventh century Norse boat has been found to be the same as is used in these craft today.

This type of very basic boat has spread and is found in many places *(Plate 51)*. Scottish and Icelandic rowing boats are built this way. There are Irish lake boats that might just as well have been Scandinavian. Skiffs of generally similar form are found in Canada and the USA. Sometimes there is a small transom instead of a rounded pointed stern.

The arrangement of a small transom at the bow instead of a pointed stem is a comparatively modern idea in northern Europe. We now call such a boat, a 'pram,' which is more correctly 'praam' in Scandinavia. A Norwegian boat of this type was of different form and had no bow board. Instead all of the planks met at a point at gunwale level. At the waterline this gave a spoon-shaped form. Instead of a keel, there was slightly stouter central plank.

The pram form used by other countries had a small bow transom. This allowed a stronger construction and avoided the problem of joining a number of planks thinned down almost to points *(Plate 52)*. The central plank instead of a hog and keel assembly was used. Providing the bow board was well above the water there was no reason why a pram should not perform well. One advantage of the Norwegian or other form was the ability to go bow first on to a beach.

In any type of boat with clinker planking there is the problem of what to do with the overlapping planks at the ends. One way is to notch the transom so that the overlap continues. This can be done at both ends on a pram dinghy. The Dutch have always built pram work and pleasure boats for their inland waters in this way, using broad oak planks in a similar way to Norwegian construction. If there is a stem, the planks have to be treated in a different way, as the ends have to be all brought to the same level against the stem post. One way is to bevel the overlapping planks, so that the bevel is progressively twisted in its length. This was done when the only available tools were not very sophisticated. In more recent construction, with the better tools of the last two centuries, it has been more usual to rebate (or 'rabbet') the under plank so that the upper plank came down to the level of the under one.

It is obviously simpler, if a tool for rebating is available, to do the same at the transom and let the outline of the transom be a smooth curve. This has been the more usual method with the narrow planking of British clinker boats.

Although the Viking influence has persisted throughout the centuries and broad-planked widely-framed boats of a utilitarian rather than a class finish are still being made in Scandinavia, and shown at the British and other European boat shows, it has been the British tradition of clinker boat building which has spread more and more to other countries.

For most of the last one hundred years, until the coming of glass reinforced plastic, the accepted yacht's dinghy has been clinker-built, with planks no more than 4in at their widest, made of mahogany in the best craft, spruce where lightness was important, or of elm or larch, where toughness and cheapness were important. Inside were bent frames at about 6in spacing, usually made of rock elm. The stem would be oak or other hardwood, while mahogany made the best transom. Mahogany made the thwarts and any trim of the boat. Finished in varnish, this made a very pretty craft. Even up to the outbreak of the 1939/45 war there were many craftsmen producing these boats at £1 per foot of length, i.e. a 10ft (3m) dinghy for £10.

The simplest fastening for clinker planking was to drive a nail through from outside and turn the point over, while an iron block was held against the head. This method of clenching the nail gave the alternative name of 'clench planking.' In cheap constructions this was done with galvanized nails, but hammering damaged the galvanizing (zinc plating) and rust occurred.

In better construction, copper nails (usually square section) were used with conical washers, called 'roves.' The rove had a hole just too small to push over the nail. The nail was driven through from outside the boat, then the head supported with an iron block. A worker inside used a hollow punch, called a 'roving iron,' to drive a rove on to the nail end. The nail end was cut off above the rove, then light hammer blows used to spread this over the rove, to make a tightly riveted joint. The blows had to be light, otherwise the soft copper nail would buckle in the thickness of the wood and might straighten again later under load and cause a leak. Longer nails went through the bent frames as well as the planking, and very long nails went through knees and other reinforcing parts. Until the development of fully waterproof glues during the 1939/45 war, all of the parts of such a boat were put together dry, the strength being provided by the riveted nails and waterproofness by the closeness of the fit, coupled with the swelling of the wood when it became wet.

Any northern European boats built with carvel planking tended to have thicker planks than those built on the Mediterranean shores. Either the Mediterranean craftsmen were more skilled at making a watertight joint between thinner planks meeting on their edges or in the warmer climate they were more willing to accept slight leaks.

Carvel planking for northern boats was, and still is, at least ⅝in thick and the edges arranged to meet for about one-third of the thickness on the inside, with a slight V to the outside. Strands of cotton were twisted and driven lightly into the bottom of the V with a caulking tool, having a broad end like a blunt chisel. This was followed by a mastic of some sort. Boat builders had their own preferences for mixtures of tar, tallow and resins. Today, the filling may be cotton or a plastic alternative and there are prepared caulking compounds of plastic base with mineral fillings.

The Dutch have been almost the only nation to use steel plate for small craft. Where other nations would not consider steel as suitable for craft less than about 50ft (15m) length, the Dutch have used steel sheet about ⅛in (3mm) thick to rivet and weld into quite small craft. Working craft only about 15ft (4.5m) long have been made with near flat

bottoms and double- or multi-chine sides made up with these plates, either with a stem or a pram bow. Such a craft is not handicapped much by its weight if it is always kept afloat, and the construction means that it is able to stand up to rough usage and abuse.

The only other metal used for boats is aluminium alloy. This has found little favour in Europe, but there have been developments in this material in America and Australia.

The development of fully waterproof glues during the 1939/45 war made possible the manufacture of plywood which could be used for boat skins. All plywood made previous to that was liable to delaminate if it became wet. As plywood sheets cannot be bent into compound curves, plywood boats had to be designed to allow for curves in the length of a panel and straight lines in transverse sections, hence the 'hard chine' and 'double chine' sections seen in many post-war amateur and professionally built boats. Marine-grade plywood in Britain is made to what must be the best-known British Standard Specification 'BSS 1088.'

Plywood boats have been made with lengthwise strips at the joints, with everything bedded in synthetic resin glue. Fastenings are mainly to hold the joints close while the glue sets. Boats have been built without fastenings other than glue, but there are then complications of cramping. Although brass or gunmetal screws have been the usual fastenings, barbed ring nails, which drive in but resist pulling out, allowed quicker assembly—important with some glues that have a comparatively short setting time.

An alternative method of plywood construction used joints made with glassfibre and resin. This is probably best-known in the *Mirror* sailing dinghy, but it was also developed for many other craft and has been particularly successful with plywood canoes. The edges are drawn together, usually with copper wire through holes, although some construction uses plastic fishing line. Resin and glassfibre tape is then put on the inside. When the resin has set, the wire projections are cut off outside and another layer of glassfibre tape in resin put there. A second layer may be added, and some craft have had the whole of the outside sheathed in glassfibre mat.

During the war some aircraft, notably the *Mosquito,* were built with layers of wood veneer bonded with synthetic resin glue. This technique was adopted for boats after the war, and Fairey Marine, an offshoot of an aircraft firm, made thousands of boats this way for about two decades until they had to give way to cheaper production in glassfibre. For 'laminated veneer' construction there has to be a mould in the shape of the boat. Over this strips of veneer are laid. The strips may be quite thin for a canoe or rowing racing shell or 1/8in (3mm) or more for a larger craft. Another layer is put over this in the other direction and bedded in glue. In light construction it is usual to hold the second layer with office staples, driven with a 'trigger tacker.' When the glue has set, the staples are withdrawn and a third layer of veneers laid, diagonally or lengthwise. When that glue has set, the staples in the outer layer are withdrawn and the surface cleaned off, then the hull removed from the mould. Staple holes are closed up by wiping the surface with hot water. In effect, this is making a piece of plywood in the shape of a boat, resulting in a very light hull that needs little internal structure.

During the 1950s the coming of glassfibre as a boat building material revolutionized boat construction. This is more suitable for quantity production than for individual boat building. Consequently, there is a greater uniformity about boats in use today. This may be an advantage in competitive boating, but much of the pride of individuality of boats has had to go *(Plate 53)*. A glassfibre (more correctly 'glass reinforced plastic or GRP') hull is an homogeneous mass, which is without joints, so the old familiar excuse for water in the bilges that 'all boats leak' has had to be abandoned.

Boats of generally similar form to the wooden craft that have gone before are now made in glassfibre and used for similar purposes. Glassfibre gets its strength from a curved form without abrupt angles, so what were angular parts on wooden boats are given curves. There are many glassfibre craft around based on plywood or clinker originals. For the new materials these are bad designs, as the chine angles in plywood craft and the many angles of the overlapping clinker planks could be weak points unless well-rounded. It is likely that as design in the new material progresses, this evidence of the influence of other materials will die out.

While glassfibre is gaining ground and about three-quarters of the craft afloat today are made of that material, many amateur-built craft are still made of plywood and craftsmen still build by traditional clinker and carvel methods. However, it is likely that skills in these other materials will be lost and glassfibre will become almost the only acceptable material for small craft.

The peak of rowing glory must have been seen in the crews of state barges. Enormous craft were used in Venice and elsewhere, but in Britain several less-massive craft still survive. Queen Mary's Shallop was built by

Plate 53. Modern glass reinforced plastic dinghy.

William III for Queen Mary II in 1689. It was used as recently as 1912 when King George V and Queen Mary attended the Royal Regatta at Henley and again for their peace pageant in 1919.

A state barge carried a few important people with due pomp and ceremony with a large number of uniformed oarsmen. There are still Royal Watermen, but their duties are more concerned with ceremonies ashore. Prince Frederick's Barge was built in 1732 by the eldest son of George II and Queen Caroline. This very ornate barge was pulled by 22 oarsmen and had enclosed accommodation for the passengers *(Plate 54)*. Aft of that was an elaborately carved poop for the steersman

(Plate 55). The underwater shape was very much on wherry lines.

Queen Mary's shallop is a smaller boat, pulled by eight oarsmen. It was built of oak and had only a semi-enclosed passenger space at the stern *(Plate 56)*. Prince Frederick's Barge was taken out of service in 1849, so Queen Mary's shallop is the last remaining barge of the British royal crown. Both of these barges are now at the National Maritime Museum at Greenwich.

It is interesting to compare western state barges with those in countries where paddling is preferred to rowing. In Thailand (Siam) very ornate state barges have canoe-shaped hulls and the passengers travel in a shelter near the

Plate 54. *Aft part of Prince Frederick's barge. This was rowed double banked with twenty-two oars. (Nat. Maritime Museum).*

Plate 55. *Carved poop and tiller on Prince Frederick's barge.*

Plate 56. Passenger accommodation on Queen Mary's Shallop. This was last used in 1919, and is the last remaining Royal Barge.

Plate 57. A Siamese State Barge. Passengers sit in the centre.

Plate 58. Figurehead on Siamese State Barge, still used by the King.

Plate 59. Passenger craft at Benares, on the Ganges in India.

middle *(Plate 57)*. Figureheads play an important part. That on a barge 169ft (50m) long and still used once a year by the king, towers about 15ft (4.6m) above the water *(Plate 58)*. A state barge uses a large number of oarsmen to propel a small number of passengers. At the other extreme, on the broad shallow waters of the Ganges, in India, two oarsmen manage to propel a double-decked load of passengers *(Plate 59)*.

CHAPTER 8

Ships boats

So long as the size of a boat was within the limits of being dragged ashore by its crew, there was no need for any other smaller craft to provide communication between it and the land. The Viking craft could be manhandled up a beach. Many of the galleys and Egyptian craft of the Mediterranean and the River Nile could be got ashore on rollers. Those that were too heavy to be easily pulled out were of sufficiently shallow draught to come close in. As the size of seagoing craft increased there had to be another smaller boat provided, so that in places where the larger craft had to moor or anchor away from the shore, this could be used as a tender to ferry people and goods. A secondary purpose of this craft might be as a life-boat for use in emergency, but there seems little evidence of early ship's boats being equipped especially for this purpose *(Plate 60)*.

There are Biblical references to craft large enough to have one or more boats, either on board or towed astern. There are also references to a further use of the boat in what is now called 'kedging'—taking out the anchor in the boat so that it can be dropped in a position where the larger craft can use it to hold off shore or pull in a direction required.

The boats used as tenders in these early days would have been similar to the small craft used in harbours and off the coast. A smaller ship might have no room on board for the boat and have to tow it astern, as is often done with a yacht's dinghy today, but a boat astern can be a nuisance, particularly in a following sea, so it would be got on board if possible. This might have been merely by lifting by sufficient helpers, but as ships were equipped with sail, the boat would probably be hauled up on a boom and swung inboard.

In more recent times fishing trawlers and craft have used a fairly heavy transom-stern boat as a tender and lifted and launched this in a very similar way.

In the days of sail, before the coming of steam, particularly as ships got larger, several boats were carried as necessities for handling the ship in a calm or getting her in and out of harbour. The ship's boats would serve somewhat similar functions to modern tugs, towing the ship as well as pushing and manoeuvring her into a harbour berth. They were also used to carry out anchors for kedging or mooring. Often the only way of getting a sailing ship out of harbour or off a lee shore was by towing with her boats or by kedging—an anchor was taken out by boat to the limit of the cable and lowered. The ship then hauled out to it while another anchor was taken out a further stage and the process repeated, slowly getting the ship in the desired direction by a series of short steps.

Plate 60. A Royal Naval Sailing Association 14, one of the last clinker built dinghies. This one was built in 1937.

76

Plate 61. A Montague whaler alongside R.S.S. Discovery *on the Thames.*

Boats carried on a sailing ship obviously bore a family resemblance to the harbour and beach boats of the country to which the ship belonged. Those carried on British and most northern European ships were fairly heavily clinker-built. Many of the boats were double-ended, so as to make getting on and off a shelving beach through surf as easy as possible. However, if the ship's anchor had to be carried, this and the amount of cable that had to be taken with it meant having a very buoyant stern to take the heavy weight. Normally, the anchor was not carried in the boat, but was slung over the stern of the boat, by a lashing that could be slipped easily when the dropping point was reached. For this work a broad transom was an advantage and the large boat used for this purpose was called a 'cutter' or 'pinnace'—names which survive today.

In a large sailing ship a variety of boats were carried, to suit the various jobs they might have to do. The smallest might be a dinghy of perhaps 12ft (3.6m), while the longest was called a 'long boat' and pulled by eight or ten oars, double-banked in most cases. There would have been at least one boat kept in smart condition and possibly with decorations. This would only be used by the captain or officers when on ceremonial visits to other ships or ashore. Today, a cargo ship has its 'jolly boat' used for this purpose.

In contrast to boats which were double-banked, with two oarsmen on each thwart, each pulling an oar on his own side, other ship's boats were single-banked, with only one man on each thwart, sitting on the side further from the blade of his oar. Ship's boats of this type were often called 'whalers,' although there was no connection with the whaling trade. Carrying through to the present day was the Royal Navy Montague Whaler, a double-ended boat 27ft (8.2m) long (Plate 61). A peculiarity of this boat was that it was pulled with five single-banked oars, two projecting on the port side and three on the starboard side. Despite this apparent unevenness there was no obvious tendency to wander off course, needing correction by the helmsman. The whaler could be rigged for sailing, but it was primarily a rowing boat, being rather too narrow for its length to make a good sailing hull.

In contrast to the comparatively slim whaler the double-banked cutter was a full-bodied broad-transomed boat. The Royal Navy cutter was 32ft (9.7m) long and pulled by twelve oars. Like the whaler the cutter could be sailed, but it was more often rowed. The naval whaler had metal crutches fitted in sockets on the gunwales, but the cutter had metal-lined notched rowlocks cut in a washboard fitted above the gunwales. When not being used, these could be closed by pieces called 'poppets.'

Most ship's boats now have engines, but it is usual to equip them for rowing as well. The heavy workboat type of transom-sterned craft used with trawlers and similar craft are still often propelled in harbour and around their parent craft by sculling over the stern with a long sweep.

Although longboats propelled by oars have disappeared from use as part of the equipment of a ship, some may still be found on remote islands. For instance, at Pitcairn, and similarly at Tristan da Cunha (Plate 62), longboats are pulled by ten oars. They provide the only means of getting through the surf to calling ships, which have to heave-to offshore. The helmsman uses a long sweep to control the boat in the breakers, then a rudder, held

Plate 62. Set of stamps illustrating the Tristan da Cunha boats.

alongside on a lanyard, is dropped into position as deep water is reached, then if conditions are favourable, masts are stepped and the longboat is sailed. Pitcairn has little shelter and the longboats have to be winched into sheds when not in use.

Pitcairn was settled by mutineers from the *Bounty*. Captain Bligh was set adrift by them on 28 April, 1789, in the Pacific some distance south east of Fiji. The mutineers went eastward and finally reached Pitcairn, where they burned the *Bounty* on 23 January, 1790, but they were not discovered for 18 years, when an American sealer called there. Meanwhile Bligh, with 18 men in a 23ft (7m) rowing boat, made what must have been the greatest ever voyage in such a craft. The boat was described as a launch. Very much overloaded, it had only about 7in (18cm) freeboard. Bligh navigated it westward and travelled 3,618 miles (5,800km) in 41 days to

reach Timor. A Dutch ship took him home and he was hailed as a hero when he reached Portsmouth on 14 March, 1790.

Some of the toughest rowing boats were the whale boats, carried by whaling ships and used for chasing and harpooning whales. They were double-ended and normally steered by a long oar or sweep. Sizes varied considerably. An American print of 1870 showed a beamy buoyant boat, not more than 25ft (7.6m) long, and pulled by four oars, with some decking aft and substantial rollers or a fairlead, called a 'loggerhead,' in the bow to take the line when the whale was harpooned and started to pull. British records describe whale boats up to twice this length.

At the cry of 'There she blows' from the masthead lookout, the whale boats were lowered and men jumped into them. The harpooner was in charge of a boat. He had a mate, but the rest of the crew rowed. The mate

Plate 63. A traditional dory with flat bottom and flared ends.

Plate 64. A modern version of the dory, similar to the craft Blyth and Ridgeway rowed across the Atlantic.

steered and the harpooner stood in the bow. When close enough he threw one or maybe two harpoons, preferably into the blubber just forward of the hump of the whale.

The line ran out, until checked, and the boat was towed at a high speed on a 'Nantucket sleigh ride.' Eventually the whale weakened. The line was shortened and the harpooner took over steering while his mate stood in the bow with a long lance, which he thrust and twisted into the whale until blood gushed and the whale eventually rolled over dead.

This was a hazardous occupation and the whale might upset or crush the boat. In 1851 the American *Ann Alexander* had two boats crushed by one whale, which then rammed the ship at an estimated 15 knots, holing it so she sank. The crew took to the remaining boats and were rescued by other ships.

Another ship's boat peculiar to its trade was the fishing dory used on the Grand Banks in the Atlantic off Newfoundland. The general design of the dory was not vastly different from the basic Scandinavian boat—a narrow flat bottom taken to a point at both ends, with sides flared out well and with considerable sheer to the gunwales so freeboard amidships was much less than at the ends *(Plate 63)*. Although the stem was pointed, there was a narrow stern transom coming to almost a point at the bottom.

There was little permanent internal structure and large numbers of these dories were carried nesting in piles on the deck of the parent ship. A central thwart and other gear were fitted to prepare the boat for use. A dory was handled by an individual fisherman. With many others he was left scattered over the ocean to catch fish and picked up some time later by the parent ship.

Although flat-bottomed craft are not generally considered to be suitable for open sea work, these Banks dories or Gloucester dories proved capable of doing their jobs. They were rowed by a pair of oars and fishing was over one side amidships. The narrow bottom and great flare to the sides, gave the tilted boat more of the effect of a V bottom, so there was not the dangerous tendency to pound in waves which there is with broad flat-bottomed boats *(Plate 64)*.

It is only in comparatively recent years that much thought has been given to the use of ship's boats as life-boats. With the development of steamers in increasing sizes and the emphasis given to the problem by some major disasters, the saving of the lives of passengers and crews in an emergency had to become the subject of legislation by the maritime nations. Little thought had been given to the use of life-boats in the days of sailing passenger ships.

Life-boats have to be provided in sufficient number to carry all the persons on board the ship. There would also be a number of rafts and floats. Although the boats have to comply with regulations of the country with which the ship is registered, many variations are possible. However, ship's life-boats have developed to a recognisable pattern. Nearly all have been very full-section, pointed at both ends, but very bluff. A life-boat of this shape was more of a load-carrier than a hull capable of progressing through the water at more than a very slow pace.

Because of the problems of launching, life-boats were never very large, but a length around 30ft (9m) has become usual. This, with its equipment and all the people it was designed to carry, might approach 20 tons (20,000kg) to be lowered down the ship's sides.

Until the coming of glassfibre, the majority

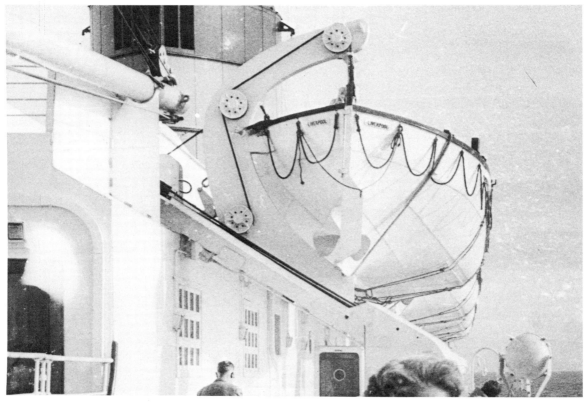

Plate 65. A life-boat in davits on the old Queen Mary.

of ship's life-boats were clinker-built. As most of them spent their whole lives high on a boat deck exposed to the weather and were rarely put afloat, they dried out and were liable to leak badly when launched. Clinker hulls, of traditional construction, are better kept afloat or frequently used so the planks soak up water and the wood swells to close joints. Other life-boats were carvel-built and the driest were double-diagonal planked in the same way as shore life-boats. Metal life-boats were also made, and these were less liable to damage if they bumped the side of the ship during launching. Today, glassfibre, laid up to a

fairly stout and heavy section, produces life-boats, still of much the same tubby shape, but almost maintenance-free and watertight, with a much longer serviceable life.

Launching methods for life-boats have exercised man's ingenuity and those used today are not foolproof. If a ship in distress heels, it may only be possible to use the boats on one side. There are still instances of boats dropping unevenly or tipping out their passengers when launched.

Davits are used to launch or recover a life-boat. The type in use for a long time consisted of two overhanging arms, spaced so

Plate 66. Sea Scouts in gigs. These craft have open gunwales, common in American craft, but rare in Britain.

that the boat could be swung from inboard to outboard. The life-boat had strong attachment points towards each end and above the keel. Chains or cables in the boat had quick-release hooks above these points for attachment to the falls from the davits. The boat was lowered, either by hand or power and the boat crew worked the release mechanism when they hit the water.

More recent arrangements use the gravity davit. With this the boat is always at the outside of the davit. Mechanism is used to swing the davit outward, then the boat is lowered by falls *(Plate 65).*

In the era of large yachts with wealthy owners, in Victorian and Edwardian days, the boats that were used as tenders were very fine examples of the boatbuilder's craft. Yachtsmen followed naval customs and the boats were comparable, although lighter and more smartly finished. The owner had his gig *(Plate 66),* which was comparable to a naval whaler, but with a small transom, in which his uniformly-dressed crew rowed him and his guests ashore.

Mahogany was the popular wood and these boats were normally bright with varnish. Even after the coming of reliable engines, the owner

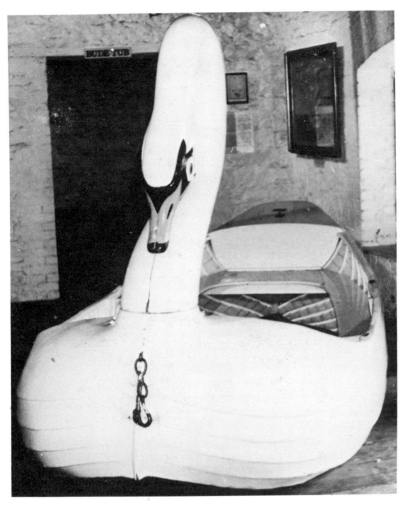

Plate 67. A bit of Victorian whimsy. This dinghy, called 'Cygnet,' was tender to a yacht called 'Swan.'

who could afford it, had his gig's crew to use as something of a status symbol. A few of these beautiful craft still survive *(Plate 67)*.

In more recent times the less wealthy yachtsman, with a smaller yacht and no paid crew tended to favour a clinker stem dinghy of about 10ft (3m) length. This would carry up to three and some equipment between anchored yacht and the shore in sheltered waters. If the parent yacht was small, the tender was more likely to be a pram dinghy as short as 7ft (2m). This would carry two and stores, but was just about the smallest suitable craft and the ferrying trip between the moorings and the shore was often the most hazardous part of a yachting expedition.

These craft were made in large numbers and sold as 'yacht's dinghies' at remarkably low prices, but despite their utilitarian design and intention, they were beautiful in the sense

Plate 68. A typical inflatable dinghy, suitable for rowing or driving with an outboard motor.

of fitness for purpose. These were the normal yacht tenders for the whole of the first half of the twentieth century.

A wooden dinghy was usually too heavy to carry on board many yachts, so it was towed astern. In some cases it was hauled on board and stowed upside-down on the cabin top. With a wooden dinghy there was always a problem of fendering. Both the dinghy and the parent craft were liable to knock each other and cause dents, so arranging satisfactory fendering was always an owner's problem. The glassfibre dinghies of generally similar form which followed the wooden dinghies in the 1950s still presented this problem, but these have been followed by inflatable dinghies, which have solved this and other problems, while bringing a few of their own.

The satisfactory performance of inflatable dinghies used by airmen who came down in the sea during the war showed the possibilities of these craft. However, these and playboats made after the war, were rubberized fabric, which is neither strong nor durable. Tough synthetic rubberlike materials have been developed, which are very difficult to damage and are immune to attack by most chemicals that affect natural rubber. These synthetic rubbers have been impregnated into fabrics, and inflatable dinghies of this laminated material used by yachtsmen have shown that they will stand up to normal uses.

The ditched airman's dinghy was able to keep him afloat, but it was not intended that he should propel it far. An inflatable yacht tender has more of a boat shape and is usually given a folding wooden floor. This gives a rigid base to stand on and stiffens the bottom so that the boat passes easier through the water. Buoyancy is provided by an inflatable ring, but this is divided into compartments, to retain some buoyancy if part is punctured. The rowlocks are made of synthetic material mounted on the side tubes. Oars are often sectional, for compact packing when the boat is stowed in its bags.

The very buoyant inflatable boat sits on the surface of the water, may blow about, and does not 'carry its way' (keep going between strokes) as well as a solid dinghy. The rowing position, sitting in the bottom of the boat, does not allow very powerful strokes. Where a solid dinghy is best rowed with long slow strokes, an inflatable is better driven by short sharp strokes.

By its nature an inflatable dinghy is one larger fender, so it does no damage by bumping into the parent craft *(Plate 68)*. It is inclined to give a rather damp ride to its crew. Most yachtsmen tend to keep their inflatable dinghy blown up, and either tow it or have it on the cabin top. When it is known that it will not be needed for some time, it can be deflated and packed away. Inflation is normally by a foot bellows.

Although inflatable boats used as yacht's tenders are normally inflated by air, it is possible to have them arranged to inflate automatically from a carbon dioxide cartridge. There are inflatable life-rafts that operate in this way, but these are mainly a means of keeping survivors afloat while they await rescue, rather than craft which can be used to go anywhere. However, self-inflating life-rafts give the yachtsman his equivalent of a life-boat, and these appliances are finding a place on larger craft in addition to normal life-boats.

While glassfibre has largely taken over from wood and inflatable craft have found most favour with yachtsmen, there is one other material that is beginning to provide an alternative. This is ABS plastic, which is not as rigid as glassfibre. Boats are being made in this material, usually with a double skin and plastic foam or air between. The material is only suitable for mass-production. As the original plant is expensive and related to the size of the product, boats produced so far have been rather small. However, the material is softer than wood or glassfibre, and boats made of ABS plastic may yet prove themselves as yacht tenders.

There was an attempt to produce boats in polystyrene foam, which is cheap and very buoyant, but it is soft and easily dented. Although such a boat might have a reasonable life, considering its low price, it had to be made quite thick (2in (5cm) or more) so it looked clumsy. With the surface damage that soon developed, coupled with the amount of dirt which penetrated the surface, a polystyrene boat soon became quite ugly. Unless further developments get over these problems it seems improbable that polystyrene small craft will ever be acceptable.

CHAPTER 9

Coastal life-boats

Earning a living from the sea, whether crossing oceans or fishing close in shore, has always been a hazardous occupation. There has always been a traditional fellowship of the sea. If a seaman was in danger of his life, all other seamen would do whatever was possible to help. Salvage and profiting from wrecks may have been a different matter, but no-one was likely to risk the lives of fellow seafarers by deliberately causing wrecking.

Early rescue attempts must have been in local fishing and work boats, but there are records of people in particular localities maintaining boats to help shipwrecked mariners long before there was any national organisation. Possibly the oldest purpose-built life-boat in the world—certainly the oldest still in existence—is the *Zetland*, which is preserved at Redcar. This double-ended clinker-built boat about 35ft (11m) long was pulled by five pairs of oars and steered with two sweeps. The bottom has a very rockered keel, possibly for getting on and off beaches through surf. The *Zetland* was built in 1800 and was used to save over 500 lives *(Plate 69)*.

Whitby is a port that still supports both fishing and boatbuilding industries. They are known to have had a life-boat station as early as 1802. From then until 1861 the people of Whitby maintained two life-boats at their own expense. In that year on 9 February several ships were in distress off Whitby at the same time. The town had a new life-boat, which went out at least five times and brought back the crews of these ships, then only a short distance from the piers she overturned and every member of the crew was drowned, except Henry Freeman, who was wearing a cork lifebelt, something only recently designed by Captain Ward, Inspector of Life-boats of the Royal National Life-boat Institution. As a result of this loss, Whitby resolved to join the RNLI and a new self-righting life-boat was put on station there in April 1861, with Henry Freeman as her first coxswain.

The first life-boat station in Britain, and probably in the world, was at Bamburgh, Northumberland. A bishop, who died in 1721 left money to set up a trust to make arrangements there to help shipwrecked mariners. A London coachbuilder, named Lionel Lukin had been experimenting with what he called an 'unimmergible' boat. Dr John Sharp, who was administrator of the trust, persuaded Lukin to use his ideas to convert a coble for use as a life-boat at Bamburgh. Lukin fitted a cork gunwale and added cork buoyancy compartments. This boat served at Bamburgh for several years.

As a result of a public outcry when the *Adventurer* was wrecked off the mouth of the Tyne and many people ashore watched those

Plate 69. An oared life-boat puts to sea.

Plate 70. The 'Bedford' life-boat, built in 1886, and only withdrawn from service in 1930. Note the cork buoyancy band round the gunwales.

on board drown without being able to help them, a competition was arranged locally for the design of a life-boat. The parish clerk was given half the prize for his ideas, which were improved by the committee and given to a local boatbuilder, named Greathead, to build. This was the *Original;* the first boat to be purpose-built as a life-boat. It was 30ft (9m) and rowed with six pairs of oars. Both gunwale and keel line rose well at the ends. Cork was used around the gunwales *(Plate 70),* as a lining and in casings. The first boat was launched in 1790. Greathead made more than thirty of these boats, which were paid for by charities and then manned and administered locally.

In 1823 Sir William Hillary, of the Isle of Man, made a case for a national life-boat service in a pamphlet. In the following year, with the aid of a London MP, named Wilson, a meeting was called and the 'National Institution for the Preservation of Life from Shipwreck' was formed. Thirty years later the name was changed to the 'Royal National Life-boat Institution.' This was a voluntary body, with funds raised from donations, legacies and other gifts. Except for a short period towards the end of the nineteenth century when government money was accepted, the Institution has continued in this way. Funds were extremely small for some time, but today this is a vast organisation dealing in millions of pounds.

There were other life-boats, all rowed *(Plate*

Plate 71. An early rescue bid about 1850, in an oared life-boat.

71). Lionel Lukin produced a 40ft (12m) boat for the Suffolk Humane Society suitable for searching in the outlying sandbanks off the east coast. She was launched in 1807, remained in service for 43 years and saved upwards of 300 lives. Another successful design was produced by the inland boatbuilder, Pellew Plenty, of Newbury. His boats looked something like a Norfolk wherry and had scuppers or draining valves to release water. He built twelve of these for the Institution.

George Palmer, a member of the committee of the Institution, designed a boat that became their standard for a quarter of a century. These 26ft 8in (9m) boats had plenty of air cases and there were scuppers to drain off water. They could be steered by rudder or sweep and had a sail to supplement the oars. Boats of this type were also built in France and used off their coast.

Although there were many designs produced, the Institution felt that not enough progress was being made and a competition was arranged in 1850. This mid-Victorian period was the time of fantastic inventions and some strange life-boats were suggested. Out of 280 entries, 50 were displayed at the Great Exhibition. Judging was on a points system and the winner was James Beeching, of Yarmouth, getting 84 out of a possible 100, indicating that the judges thought his design could be improved *(Plate 72)*

A boat to Beeching's design was built. This

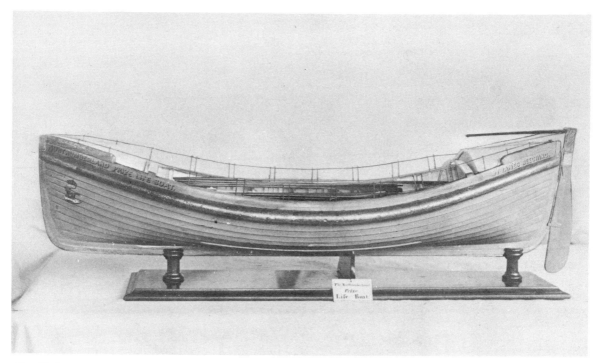

Plate 72. James Beeching's prize design, 1851.

was 36ft (11m) long, with a beam of 9½ft (2.5m), rowed with six pairs of oars. A 6in (15cm) wide cork fender ran around just below the gunwales. There were air cases inside. In the bottom was a water tank, divided into compartments, for ballast. Tubes through the bottom allowed water taken in to be drained out. There were high air cases fore and aft and an iron keel as well as the water ballast. The total weight was over 3 tons (3,000kg) and quite a lot for the oarsmen to propel, but the important thing was that the combination of high buoyancy and heavy keel weight made her self-righting in the event of a capsize.

James Peake, a member of the Institution committee, took Beeching's design and built a lighter version 30ft (9m) long, pulled by five pairs of oars and weighing just over 2 tons (2,000kg). She was found to free herself of water through non-return valves in the drain tubes in 55 seconds and would right herself in 5 seconds after being inverted by a crane.

Between 1851 and 1887 most effort was concentrated on perfecting self-righting life-boats, but there were other types. A father and son, named Richardson, produced a boat made of two iron tubes 40ft (12m) long and 2½ft (75cm) diameter, placed 3ft (90cm) apart. This was rowed from a platform with netting around it mounted on the tubes. This boat was stationed at Rhyl in 1856. Seven years later another like it was located at New Brighton and remained there for 35 years. One service it did was rescue the crew of

Plate 73. The Padstow oared life-boat.

another tubular life-boat belonging to the Liverpool Harbour Board in 1875 *(Plate 73).*

Not all life-boatmen were convinced that self-righting craft were the best. One not self-righting of the period was the Cromer type, built in 1884. This was 35ft (10.5m) long, 10ft (3m) beam and pulled fourteen oars. Two years later there was a disaster which strengthened the call for self-righting boats.

This was the wreck of the *Mexico* off Southport, Lancashire, on 9 December, 1886. A full gale was blowing and the crew of the Southport life-boat was called out. Horses took the boat 3½ miles (5.75km) along the coast, where it was launched. The life-boat was close to the ship, when she capsized. Two hours later the life-boat was washed ashore

with two of her crew clinging to her. The other thirteen had been drowned. The St Annes life-boat had also been called out. What happened to her is not known, but all of the crew were drowned. The Lytham boat had also been called out. This was a new life-boat on her first service. She filled several times and three oars were broken, but by using the anchor, the life-boat veered alongside and the crew of the ship were taken off and successfully got ashore. However, 27 life-boatmen lost their lives that night.

One result of that disaster was increasing awareness of the life-boat service by the general public and much greater financial help. Life-boats were paraded through the streets and this was really the start of the

92

Plate 74. A life-boat launch from a carriage.

annual life-boat flag days which allow the man in the street to contribute towards the service.

Although many life-boats of the end of the nineteenth century had sails as well as oars, the muscle power of the crews was most important. The conditions in which a life-boat would be called out were often not suitable for sailing. The same man who rowed had to do whatever was necessary at a wreck, then return with a loaded boat. Most crews were fishermen and volunteers. The Institution has never had many fulltime crew men. Even today, with the complexities of modern powered life-boats, there is usually only one fulltime man at each station. Other crew get a payment when they are on service or exercise,

but this is only nominal *(Plate 74)*.

By the turn of the twentieth century steam engines had come into shipping and there were some steam life-boats. The internal combustion engine was coming in and the first to be fitted to a life-boat was in 1904. This phase brought the era of pulling life-boats towards a close, although individual boats continued to give good service for a long time. An Aberdeen boat (not then part of the RNLI) had no motor as late as 1920.

Of course there are many stories of bravery of life-boatmen and of feats which would have been regarded as impossible, if they were not known to have actually happened. Besides the events at sea there have been some fantastic ones ashore. The Whitby life-boat, under the

Plate 75. An oared life-boat in heavy seas.

survivor Henry Freeman, was taken overland from Whitby to Robin Hood's Bay and successfully launched to help a ship in distress there. This involved hills, both up and down, as well as moors.

Even more unbelievable was the taking of the Lynmouth life-boat to Porlock over Exmoor. Holidaymakers who have followed this route will know that there is a mile (1.6km) of one in four and a half Countisbury Hill out of Lynmouth up to the moors, then about 10 miles (16km) across the moors to the even steeper Porlock Hill, going down one in four.

The *Forrest Hall,* a fully-rigged ship of 1,900 tons sent out distress calls during the night of 12 January, 1899, while in Porlock Bay. A telegraph message was sent to Lynmouth and the decision was made to attempt to get the life-boat there overland, as the onshore gale prevented the boat being launched at Lynmouth.

A farmer provided upwards of a dozen horses and with the help of large numbers of men and women the boat on its waggon was got to the top of Countisbury Hill, where the full force of the gale was felt. The signalman of the boat went on ahead with some helpers

Plate 76. Surf life-boat from Apollo bay, Victoria, Australia.

Plate 77. The Blythe life-boat Salford, *built 1867.*

to clear and widen the road. The life-boat crew followed with their horses and twenty helpers.

There was one stretch of a mile (1.6km) only 7ft (2m) wide. This had been anticipated. The boat was got off the waggon, and was drawn through on skids, which had to be constantly picked up and carried forward again. All of this was being done at night with only the light of flares and lanterns *(Plate 75)*.

With all the restraints that could be managed, the boat and waggon were got down Porlock Hill. At the bottom the boat was too wide to get between two cottages and these had to be partly knocked down to get it through. An account says that the occupants, woken in the early hours of the morning, agreed. Someone must have been persuasive.

Without waiting for food the life-boatmen got afloat and reached the *Forrest Hall* 10½ hours after leaving Lynmouth and nearly 24 hours after she had sent out her calls. By then a steam paddle tug had also been summoned. The life-boat was able to assist the tug in getting the ship off and she was towed across to Barry.

Of such stuff are the life-boatmen made.

In recent years coastal lifesaving needs have changed. The RNLI now have many outboard motor-powered inflatable rescue craft, concerned mainly with rescuing swimmers in trouble or people in small craft. Surf lifesaving has also called for special craft. In some places a type of surfboard with a seat has been found successful for quickly getting through the surf with the aid of a double-bladed paddle. At many Australian surfing beaches and at a few British beaches there are light trolley-launched pulling boats, steered with a sweep. To achieve lightness with strength, many of these are moulded veneer construction *(Plates 76 and 77)*.

CHAPTER 10

European canoes and kayaks

Unrelated to other European craft, but very much part of the European boating scene are kayaks, which are often rather confusedly described as canoes in Europe. Although they have spread to other parts of the world their origin is British. Although these decked craft, propelled with double-bladed paddles, have a certain likeness to Eskimo kayaks, they really stem from an idea by John MacGregor. He had been to North America and he may have seen kayaks there. He was well-off, a barrister, philanthropist and something of a character.

Canoes or kayaks, as recreational craft, did not exist in Britain, but John MacGregor designed his own canoe and had it built by Searle's of Lambeth in 1865. It was 15ft 6in (4.6m) long and 2ft 6in (76cm) beam, clinker-built with oak planking. The decking was cedar and there was a cockpit about 4ft (1.2m) long. It had a double-bladed paddle about 7ft (2m) long, and the boat was equipped with a mast and simple sail. Altogether this weighed about 90lb (41kg). MacGregor called the canoe *Rob Roy*, and this became the generally-used name for the type of craft and may still be heard at boat hirers.

MacGregor toured extensively *(see Chapter 12)* and wrote about these voyages. Considerable interest was aroused. Many other similar canoes were built, mainly by fairly wealthy people. The Canoe Club was formed. The Prince of Wales (later King Edward VII) was interested and the club became the Royal Canoe Club. This club is still the premier canoe club in Britain and they have their clubhouse at Trowlock Island, a short distance above Teddington Lock on the River Thames. The original *Rob Roy* canoe is still preserved there.

Many other canoeists experimented with their craft and by the beginning of the twentieth century the rather upper-class interest in canoeing was turning towards sailing. Warington Baden-Powell, the eldest brother of the founder of the Scout Movement, was a leader in this move, and sailing canoes developed to become the fastest sailing machines in the world—a position they held until catamarans beat them in the 1950s. One result of this sailing interest was that there was very little paddling done. The fastest sailing canoes were unsuitable for paddling, in any case. Paddling canoeing did not die, but it was not until the 1920s that interest in it began to revive in Britain.

There is a story that a German professor decided to visit a museum on a wet Sunday. He closed his umbrella as he went in, then saw an Eskimo kayak. He wondered if it would be possible to make a craft like that which would fold like his umbrella. This was supposed to

Plate 78. A British scout kayak of about 1930.

be the birth of the folding canoe. More factually, a master tailor named Johann Klepper made the first 'faltboot' (foldboat) in 1907 at Rosenheim, Bavaria, Germany. The products of the Klepper factory have been considered to be amongst the finest folding craft ever since. They have been used for many lengthy and adventurous voyages *(see Chapter 12)*.

Other firms started making folding canoes, the majority being in Germany, with a few in France and elsewhere. Amateurs made rigid canoes with canvas skins, but little of this movement was felt in Britain at first. The 'Boy's Own Paper' contained occasional instructions for making rigid canvas canoes throughout the period, but there was little popular interest.

In 1929 the Scout Associations of the world held a giant Jamboree at Birkenhead to celebrate the coming of age of the movement. A contingent of scouts from Hungary gave a mass canoeing display on a reservoir, using simple canvas-covered rigid decked canoes. This was the first time that canoes in quantity had been seen in Britain. The British magazine 'The Scouter' published instructions for building similar craft and this may be regarded as the start of greater interest in modern canoeing in Britain. The author of this book was at the Jamboree and made his first canoe to this design in 1930 *(Plate 78)*.

Folding canoes were mostly professionally-made. They differed in details, but basically they had a rubber and canvas ply hull, sewn to a canvas deck arranged to fit to a wooden cockpit coaming. The framework was assembled in two parts, which were pushed into the skin via the cockpit opening *(Plate 72)*. The two parts were joined and a

Plate 79. A folding canoe being assembled.

Plate 80. A canvas covered rigid canoe.

Plate 81. A canoe framework.

tensioning arrangement forced the framework tight in the skin and locked the parts together. Parts packed into two bags; one like a large rucksack and one like a large golf bag.

Rigid kayak-type canoes were, and still are, mostly amateur products and made with a framework of widely-spaced laths on frames, covered at first with canvas, painted after fitting, but more recently covered with plastic-impregnated fabric *(Plate 80)*. Such a hull is much tougher than may, at first, be imagined. Fabric gives, where a thin rigid wooden skin might crack.

As the use of cars became much more general after the 1939/45 war and the transport of rigid canoes on car roof racks became possible, interest in folding canoes waned. The big advantage of a folding canoe was that it packed into two bags that could be taken on a bus or train. The user had to allow about 30 minutes at the beginning and end of a trip on the water to assemble or dismantle

the canoe, preferably with additional time for drying *(Plate 81)*.

Although the majority of rigid canoes in the post-war years were fabric-covered, and nearly all to the 'PBK' designs of the author of this book, thin plywood also became popular. At first this was used over internal lengthwise strips, as in larger plywood craft, but the 'Kayel' system was devised by a schoolmaster, named Ken Littledyke, as glassfibre came into use towards the end of the 1950s, with plywood panels wired together and the joints covered with glassfibre tape bedded in resin. This light simple method is also found in several class sailing dinghy designs. Maybe other designers had similar ideas, but the credit for being the first with it appears to go to Mr. Littledyke.

The coming of glassfibre affected canoes in the same way as other craft, and nearly all professionally-made kayak types, both for touring and competition, are now made in this material.

CHAPTER 11

Competitive boating

Trying to go faster than the other man seems to have been the aim of boat users from the earliest days. There was a race between four Trojan galleys described in *Aeneid V* by Virgil. During the Middle Ages inland waters were used for transporting goods and people as the roads were in a bad state and impassable in bad weather. This meant that there were large numbers of professional boatmen, and they arranged races amongst themselves, probably with bets on the results. The boats used would have been their working craft.

This led to special boats and there are records of professional four-oared and eight-oared races. However, professional interest in these classes decreased and the professional concentrated on sculling. From the later part of the nineteenth century professional oarsmanship has been confined to sculling. In the language of the oarsman, 'rowing' means one oar per man, while 'sculling' is one pair of sculls (oars) pulled by one man. Professional sculling continues today.

Organised British racing has developed over the last three centuries. Dr Johnson wrote to Mrs Theale about a regatta taking place at Vauxhall, in London, in 1775. This is the first record of such an event. The word 'regatta' comes from Italy and was the name given to races on the Grand Canal in Venice. Races were held in eight-oared state barges between crews from Pisa, Genoa and Amalfi, as well as from Venice.

An interesting event, which still takes place, is the annual race on the tidal Thames for Doggett's coat and badge. Thomas Doggett was an Irishman, who became an actor and met with little success in Dublin, so he moved to London. Faulkner's 'History of Chelsea' says:

'He performed with great reputation, and by his talents, industry and economy, acquired a competent fortune and quitted the stage some years before he died. He was a Whig "up to head and ears"; and took every occasion of demonstrating his loyalty to the House of Hanover. One instance, among others, is well-known; which is, that in the year after King George the First came to the throne, in 1715, Doggett gave a waterman's orange-coloured coat and silver badge to be rowed for; on the latter is represented the Hanoverian horse; but the newspapers of the day will have it represent the wild unbridled horse of liberty. This contest takes place on the first day of August, being the anniversary of that King's accession to the throne, between six young watermen, who have just completed their apprenticeship; the claimants starting off on a signal being given at the time of the tide when the current is strongest against them, and rowing from the Old Swan near London Bridge, to the White Swan at Chelsea.'

The race is still run, basically according to the original rules and the coat and badge are still awarded, 250 and more years after the first races. The family of Phelps have had their name figure frequently amongst the annual winners.

Early British boats built specially for racing were called 'wager' boats, presumably because in professional rowing races competitors, or their backers, laid wagers on the events. One boat of that time was a 'funny.' This was a narrow double-ended sculling wager boat with outriggers, for one man. It was clinker-built and rather unsteady. It was not particularly fast and gave way to the 'whiff,' which was a long narrow outrigged sculling boat used on the Thames. This gave way, in turn, to the 'best boat.' A race in boats owned by clubs, instead of individuals was called 'rum-tum' racing, particularly if clubs lent racing craft for competition between professional watermen. At first, events between professional scullers were described as 'best and best,' meaning that each man could use the best boat he could find.

This led to special boats being built, long and narrow, with only just room for one to sit. Earlier boats had mostly been clinker, but later craft had smooth exteriors. As 'best boat' design progressed during the nineteenth century these craft became extremely light (17lb (8kg) was quoted). They had no keel except a small fin aft. The bottom was smooth and semi-circular. Giving any boat a semi-circular section reduced the wetted area, and therefore drag, to a minimum, but stability is

then negligible and the sculler has to hold himself level when at rest by using his oars in their outrigger rowlocks on the surface of the water. The sculler sat in a small area surrounded by washboards, or coaming, later usually on a sliding seat. Basically this is the form used today.

Although there have always been amateur scullers, this side of the sport has been dominated by professionals. The amateurs have developed rowing, with crews of up to eight men. The definition of 'amateur' would seem to be one who takes up an occupation for pleasure and not for money, but in rowing the meaning has had to be further defined. In 1879 the following rules concerning a rowing amateur were adopted:

'No person shall be considered an amateur oarsman or sculler: 1. Who has ever competed in any open competition for a stake, money or entrance fee; 2. Who has ever competed with or against a professional for any prize; 3. Who has ever taught, pursued, or assisted in the practice of athletic exercises of any kind as a means of gaining a livelihood; 4. Who has been employed in or about boats for money or wages; 5. Who is, or has been by trade or employment for wages, a mechanic, artisan, or labourer.'

This left amateur rowing to the few who qualified as 'gentlemen' by the definitions of the day. The rules have been eased considerably, but anyone contemplating rowing or sculling as an amateur still has to satisfy more than the simple popular definition of an amateur.

This very strict definition of 'amateur' was fostered by the Amateur Rowing Association (ARA). To cater for those who could not conform to these very strict rules, particularly

103

Plate 82. Folding canoes at Putney, being prepared for a tideway race.

Plate 83. A K2 racing canoe in the 1948 Olympic Games at Henley.

as regards their occupation, the National Amateur Rowing Association (NARA) was formed in 1890. The Women's Amateur Rowing Association (WARA) came later *(Plate 82)*.

Another term for an amateur, popular in Victorian days, was 'Corinthian.' This came from the name of the Corinthian Yacht Club, which was a downriver branch of the London Rowing Club, where the declared object was the encouragement of yacht and boat sailing by amateurs.

It was in the early part of the nineteenth century that amateur rowing began to be organised as a sport. The leading British rowing club, Leander (on the Thames near Kingston), was formed in 1818. School and university rowing dates from about then. Oxford and Cambridge first raced each other in 1829. That was at Henley. They moved to the Putney to Mortlake course, which is still used, in 1845. University records show that the boats were not outrigged until 1846, while the first keel-less boats were used in 1857. Sliding seats did not come in until 1873.

The straight broad stretch of the River Thames at Henley lends itself to racing and it became the premier place for regattas, the first official Henley Regatta being in 1839 *(Plate 83)*. Henley provides a lead in the rowing world and most rowing regattas are modelled on their requirements. The largest boats raced are eights. These carry a cox. Other classes are coxless. These are pair-oared boats and fours. There are also events for single and double scullers.

Outside Britain rowing has always been popular in Australia and New Zealand, developing in step with England. There is rowing in Canada, the chief club being the Argonauts of Toronto. Rowing in the USA developed in much the same way as in Britain. A race similar to the Oxford and Cambridge race is staged between Harvard and Yale Universities, the first race being in 1852.

For amateur sculling the race for the Wingfield Sculls, started in 1830, is regarded as the British amateur championship event. This is held over the university Putney to Mortlake course. A better-known sculling event is the Diamond Sculls event at Henley. This attracts entries from all over the world. Described as the most polished sculler, F. S. Kelly of Great Britain (although Australian by birth), achieved the record time of 8min 10sec in 1905.

Rowing and sculling are Olympic Games events, attracting a wide entry, with Eastern Bloc countries increasing their challenge to the West.

Propelling a boat with a pole thrusting on the bottom has only a limited following as a sport, but in some Thames regattas there are punt events. A racing punt is flat-bottomed and about 27ft (8m) long and 2ft (60cm) beam. The pole is about 16ft (4.8m). The course has to be over a length of river with a hard bottom and not too great a depth of water, so it is normally laid out parallel with and not far from a straight bank. Punting is by one man, standing near the centre of the punt. As this sort of craft is double-ended and cannot be turned easily, races are arranged up and back several times over the course, with the crew changing direction to push the other end first at each end.

Poling an open Canadian-type canoe has been tried. This is done in the same way as poling a punt, but the canoe is less stable. In Britain this has only been tackled competitively at the Royal Canoe Club at Teddington on the River Thames.

Plate 84. An all plywood white water canoe.

Although there must have been competitive canoeing amongst early users of canoes and kayaks, it is only in recent years that such events have been treated as serious sport. With its greater versatility, the canoe has been used in several different ways for sport and these have developed along their own lines. Straightforward racing, comparable to rowing, is generally known as 'sprint' racing to differentiate it from the other types. 'Long-distance' racing involves greater distances with natural obstacles to contend with. The canoe sport with most spectator interest is 'slalom' in which the canoeist fights the natural hazards of a rapid river while attempting to pass through 'gates' suspended over the water. Allied to this is 'whitewater racing,' which is popular in some countries,

and once called 'kandahar,' but with little following in Britain. Perhaps not quite a sport, but worth mentioning is 'canoe polo,' played like water polo, but in canoes. 'Canoe surfing' has been arranged competitively, but is more of a recreation than a sport *(Plate 84)*.

Sprint racing in kayaks did not begin to be taken seriously until the early 1930s, when a few enthusiasts began racing in specially-built craft in Britain, and in many European countries, particularly Germany. These early craft were slimmed-down and lengthened versions of the types then used for touring. In those days most touring was in folding canoes and some racers were folders, braced internally with wires and turnbuckles to give maximum rigidity when afloat.

There had been earlier racing, but it was

almost entirely confined to the Royal Canoe Club, on the River Thames. Some of the development of racing kayaks is due to them, but it was the efforts of German and Scandinavian designers that produced the specialist racing kayaks that were the models for those used today. Some of the best racng kayaks today come from Denmark.

Sprint racing in kayaks was introduced into the Olympic Games in 1936. It was the next Olympic Games, in Britain in 1948, that set the pattern for kayak racing. These races were held over the Henley rowing course. At that time racing kayaks were being made in a few European countries, but there were no British builders. Some racing kayaks were produced at the last moment by a British firm which had made aircraft propellers during the war, based on prototypes imported from Denmark.

Sprint racing is in single-seat craft, called 'K1,' two-seat craft, called 'K2,' and four-seat 'K4' kayaks. The greatest interest is in the single-seat kayaks, which are about 16ft (5m) long, with 20in (50cm) beam and a weight of about 26lb (12kg). To conform to international standards the exact dimensions are metric. The two-seat kayaks are 21ft (6m) long, while the four-seaters, which are not so popular, are 36ft (11m) long.

Racing kayaks for first-class competition are moulded veneer in the same way as the best sculling hulls, but for less important races and for training, many glassfibre kayaks are used. These are much cheaper and less liable to damage, but not as fast.

A racing kayak has a near semi-circular section and is decked except for a small cockpit. The paddler sits on a moulded seat, with his feet against a footrest. All racing kayaks have rudders. Various positions for the rudder have been tried and it was often put right at the stern, but it is more usually now of playing-card size under the hull a few feet in from the stern. The rudder is operated by the forward paddler, usually with a tiller over the footrest and between his feet.

Racing kayaks are comparable in many ways to rowing and sculling craft, but propelling a hull while sitting facing forward is not as mechanically efficient a way of using a man's muscle power as having him face aft and pull an oar. A racing sculling or rowing boat can normally beat a comparable paddling kayak.

Kayaks, of course, are paddled with double-bladed paddles. The equivalent racing canoes for use with single-bladed paddles are defined as 'C1' and 'C2' (Plate 85). Lengths are similar to the kayaks, but beams are greater to allow for the extra stability needed for the higher position of paddlers who rest on one knee and one foot. These canoes are open for most of their length and do not have the upswept ends of traditional Canadian canoes. A limited amount of end decking is permitted and there are no rudders. The paddle used in these craft is larger and more spadelike than those used for touring.

Canoe racing is normally over courses of 500, 1,000 and 10,000 metres. Women's and junior events are normally 500 metres. There have been several attempts at standardizing smaller kayaks for junior racing, and there are junior racing kayaks in glassfibre, to provide the necessary cheapness, but for first-class racing, juniors are more likely to use the full-size standard 'K' classes.

Long-distance racing has a considerable following in Britain. It suits the complexities of the British waterways system and can take in events on canals, rivers and harbours. Races may be only a few miles, but are more

Plate 85. A C2 racing canoe with paddlers standing, in the 1948 Olympics.

likely to be nearer twenty, with hazards along the route. A typical race would be on a river or canal, with locks to be portaged at intervals, or there might be weirs that could be either shot or portaged. Tidal long-distance races might give the option of carrying over a spit of land or paddling round.

There are long-distance races most week-ends of the year, and many club members travel the country to race. There are many trophies. The controlling body, as for all British canoeing, is the British Canoe Union.

There have been several designs produced for long-distance racing, between touring and sprint racing types, but there have been many changes of rules covering dimensions and for some long-distance races competitors now use sprint racing kayaks.

The most famous long-distance canoe race and alleged to be the most arduous in the world, is outside the normal long-distance race rules of the BCU. It is the Devizes-Westminster race which takes place every Easter and involves passage along the semi-derelict Kennet and Avon Canal from Devizes to Reading, then down the Thames to finish at the Houses of Parliament. Competitors have to choose their own starting

time to suit their estimate of the right time to pass Teddington on to the tideway and get the benefit of the tide down to Westminster. The total distance is 125 miles (200km). Of this, 54 miles (87km) (with 57 locks) are on the canal. From Reading it is 71 miles (113km) (and 20 locks) to Westminster—17 miles (27km) of this being tidal.

The history of this event is getting confused. These are believed to be the facts. A gentleman in Pewsey, near Devizes, offered £20 (then the price of a simple new canoe) to anyone who could get to London in less than 100 hours by boat. The offer was taken up by the Devizes Boy Scout Group. When the challenger said he only intended Pewsey people, a local sports club put up a larger amount for them. At Easter 1948 they took two old canvas-covered canoes along the route, paddled by four 17-year-old boys. They got to Westminster in 89 hours 50 minutes, including two overnight camps. This got publicity via the radio and national press and aroused a lot of interest.

Chippenham Sea Cadets were offered a similar sum by local supporters if they could beat the Devizes Boy Scouts. This they did at Whitsun of the same year, using two heavy commando canoes, in about 76 hours. As the canal weeded-up almost solidly in the summer, nothing further could be done that year, but at Easter 1949 about twenty teams turned up at Devizes, all determined to beat the Chippenham boys. The writer of this book, with his Alperton Sea Scouts, formed one of the teams. We all got someone to confirm our starting time, but there was no proper race organisation. The fastest time was 49 hours 32 minutes, put up by a pair of two-seaters from the Richmond Canoe Club. As a result of this Albert Weibel, of that club, offered a cup for annual competition and that was the start of the properly organized race.

The Devizes-Westminster canoe race has been held each Easter since 1950 under rules agreed by an organizing committee. The route has remained the same, but the rules have varied. Crews no longer stop at night, but for a very long time they were still expected to carry camping gear. The race has attracted entries from the services. When the fastest time came down to less than 24 hours, that was considered the limit, but in 1961 two Royal Marines, G. R. Howe and C. E. Tandy, recorded a time of 20 hours 59½ minutes, then in 1962 they reduced this to 20 hours 33 minutes.

The main event is an adult race, but from 1953 there has been a junior race with two compulsory overnight stops. Only the actual paddling times are recorded. Under these conditions the race has been paddled by junior competitors about two hours faster than the best adult times.

Canoe slalom gets its name from the snow slalom on skis and is a basically similar event. The first serious canoe slalom took place in Germany just before the 1939/45 war. In Britain there was a slalom at Llangynidr, Breconshire, on the River Usk in 1949. Canoe slalom has developed into a popular canoeing sport. As it is more of a spectacle than other canoeing, it has attracted more public interest, both as spectators on the spot and as television viewers.

A slalom takes place on a stretch of broken water. It may be a rapid river, where there are confused fast parts and currents around rocks, possibly extending for one-quarter mile. It may be below a weir on a navigable river possibly with sluices open to give a lot of turbulence below the weir. In that case the whole event takes place fairly close to the bottom of the weir. A more recent development has been the making of artificial slalom courses, or the alteration of natural ones to produce the desired hazards. This is done in some European countries and was found in Germany for the 1972 Olympic Games, the only time canoe slalom has appeared in their programme.

Except in team events a slalom canoeist is on the course alone and he races against the clock. Twenty or so 'gates' consist of poles suspended from lines above. The bottoms of the poles are on or just above the water. Gates are numbered in sequence and the poles are coloured to indicate the direction they are passed. Of course, the competitor has to deal with the water conditions at the same time.

The winner is the paddler recording the shortest time over the course, but penalty times are added to that time for touching or missing gates and other faults. Interest is such today that slalom canoeists are graded in league tables and the number of entries at a slalom may be a hundred or more. Events are held almost every weekend of the year. The use of wet-suits has made winter slalom

Plate 86. Scout canoeists enter a Thames lock during a scout cruise in the 1950's.

competition possible, when rivers are often in the best state for these events.

At first slaloms were friendly events using whatever touring canoes were available. As the sport developed rapidly in the immediate post-war years rules were made and competitors experimented with special kayaks. At that time most touring canoeists used folding craft, and an early rule stipulated that slalom craft should fold. With the coming of glassfibre this rule was discarded. Although plywood and fabric-covered slalom kayaks continued for some time, the stage has now been reached where all slalom competition is in glassfibre kayaks of special design.

A slalom kayak is a single-seater, shorter than a touring kayak, but with enough beam and flattish sections to give reasonable stability. The cockpit is as small as can reasonably be entered and the canoeist sits gripped in a shaped seat, with his knees in special grips and his feet on a rest. The hull has considerable rocker in the length so that it turns easily. With the man and canoe working as one, due to the tight fitting of the paddler in the canoe, an expert can manoeuvre on the water so as to contend with almost any condition. A spray cover is worn to prevent water entering the canoe. All first-class slalom canoeists can recover from a capsize by rolling back up or completely over. This may happen several times during a run over a slalom course.

One result of the great interest in slalom

has been the improvement of techniques, which have benefited all canoeists. Many of the double-bladed paddle techniques have been adapted from those of the Red Indian using a single-bladed paddle in his birchbark canoe *(Plate 86)*. Possibly because of this there has been an interest aroused in slalom with single-bladed paddles. At first both one and two seat craft, in glassfibre, were made with slightly rising ends in the fashion of an Indian canoe, but the paddlers knelt in cockpits arranged in decking. The upswept ends were discarded and at a quick glance slalom 'C' craft now look very much like kayaks.

Straightforward racing on rapid or whitewater rivers calls for craft better able to keep on a course than a pure slalom canoe, but still with enough manoeuvrability to negotiate rapids. Consequently canoes for this sport tend to be generally similar to slalom craft, but rather longer to give better speed and course-keeping qualities.

There is only moderate support for whitewater or rapid river racing in Britain, possibly because the rivers do not lend themselves to it in many places, but interest is increasing, to the extent that there are National Championships. This type of racing is more popular on the whitewater rivers of some European countries. The minimum acceptable length of course is 3km, but most are much longer. It is also popular in some parts of the USA. The Arkansas River Race sometimes attracts international entries. In South Africa the annual Maritzburg-Durban race adds snakes to other hazards.

Much basic canoe training takes place in swimming baths. A short canoe, generally called a 'bat,' was devised for training in these confined waters and the exceptional manoeuvrability of it was found to make it suitable for playing polo in the baths. This may never develop into a serious sport, but it has advantages as a means of teaching canoe handling, and it represents yet another sporting use of a canoe.

CHAPTER 12

Small craft voyages

Many notable journeys have been made in boats and canoes. Man has used his own muscle-power to make hazardous and long voyages over water. Many of the earlier voyages are too far back into history to be fully documented or statistically recorded. Some of these have been mentioned elsewhere in this book. Cruises by such adventurers as the Irish monks in skin boats, the Polynesians in frail canoes and the Vikings in their open boats, were fantastic and praiseworthy by any standards, but there are more recent adventurous voyages, which are fully authenticated and recorded, showing equal daring, bravery and skill.

Brief details of some of these are given in this chapter. Modern small boat voyaging does not appear to have aroused much interest until the middle of the nineteenth century. If there were earlier voyages in the last few centuries their details have not been recorded. Conquest of the seas was certainly going on and sailing ships were being used for adventurous voyages of discovery, but there are no records of small craft being used for other than utilitarian activities around the coast and in harbours.

Many small craft voyages have been underaken purely in an adventurous spirit, just for the sake of the exploit or to do something that had not been done before. In some cases the adventurer undertook his voyage to prove a point. Sometimes the small craft adventure was a necessity of war.

What seems to have started modern interest in small boat adventure was the writings of John MacGregor about his canoe trips. If he had only made the voyages and kept the details of his canoes and travels to himself, it is interesting to speculate on what effect this might have had on small boat cruising. No doubt, someone else would have started the interest moving. It is right that MacGregor's travels should come first in this listing, which is then arranged in chronological order.

Cruises of the Rob Roy

John MacGregor *(see Chapter 10)* certainly made good use of his *Rob Roy* canoe. As a wealthy man he had the time to devote to his new recreation and he was far more publicity-conscious than was usual at the time. His voyages were extensive and noteworthy, and he made sure that the public knew about them by writing for magazines and publishing books.

Paddling this sort of craft with a double-bladed paddle was something new and MacGregor was very much a pioneer. He launched his *Rob Roy* at Westminster on 9 July, 1867, and paddled down the tidal Thames to Sheerness. There it was shipped to Ostend. The first continental river was the

Sambre, then MacGregor paddled down the Mause to Liege, where he was joined by the Earl of Aberdeen in another similar canoe. They paddled to Maestricht in Holland and had their canoes taken first to the Rhine for a short trip and then to the Main. The Earl of Aberdeen left at Frankfurt and MacGregor continued alone.

These were the days before camping and MacGregor had to find accommodation every night. His passage was something of a sensation and large crowds were attracted in many places. For the safety of the canoe, it had to be taken indoors at many of the places where he slept. One man in so small a boat was very much a novelty.

MacGregor decided to canoe the Danube from the source. After canoeing on an alleged haunted lake, the *Rob Roy* was launched at Donaueschingen into the Danube. Mac-Gregor was tackling unknown waters, on a part of the river believed by the locals to be un-navigable because of rapids. People gathered to see him off each morning. His departure was even signalled by ringing church bells and firing guns.

He came through successfully and he reached Ulm, where the Danube had become a broad navigation. From there the canoe was taken to Lake Constance. It was also used on the Rhine and several other lakes. MacGregor shot the rapids on the Reuss at Bremgarten—his toughest canoeing so far. He went to the Aar and the Rhone. He tackled several other rivers before getting on to the River Marne at Epernay to travel two hundred miles to finish his trip at Paris in October.

During the four-month trip he had been sending dispatches about it to the *Record* newspaper. On his return he was called on to lecture. He even read a paper about the *Rob Roy* to the Institution of Naval Architects. He made an account of the trip into a book, '1,000 miles in the Rob Roy Canoe.' This became a best-seller immediately.

MacGregor soon followed with other voyages equally adventurous and unusual, all of which were described in books. MacGregor was what he called a 'muscular Christian.' He always carried tracts in the language of the country he was visiting. Sunday was always a rest day. On some trips he camped, but this was very different from modern camping, with servants who walked along the banks and set up camp as well as doing the cooking.

In 'Rob Roy on the Jordan' (published in 1869 and into an eighth edition by 1904) MacGregor fills twenty-four chapters in the rather ponderous Victorian way, with much about politics and people and not such a lot about canoeing. However, he went on the Suez Canal and many lakes as well as the River Jordan. It can be imagined how this Britisher in an unusual craft was even more of a sensation to Arabs than he was to Europeans. At one place he was taken prisoner, the canoe being lifted bodily from the water by swimmers with MacGregor in it. From his writings it appears that he could charm his way out of this and most situations.

For most of his canoeing MacGregor remained faithful to the paddle, but with other of his canoes later in the nineteenth century he showed he was following the bias towards sail of other canoeists, in making the canoe more of a sailing craft.

The Voyage of the Paper Boat
In the 1860s there was considerable enthusiasm for rowing in New York and efforts were made to produce increasingly lighter racing shells. Fragile cedar shells were

made down to 40lb (18kg). Elisha Waters tried laying up laminations of paper and shellac with an old wooden shell as a mould. With a little wooden framing and outriggers his shell only weighed 30lb (13.6kg). Waters was a paper box manufacturer at Troy, New York, and he obtained patents for this method of boatbuilding. The firm went into production in 1867 and the most refined racing shells went down to 22lb (10kg). These were stronger and faster than wooden shells.

By 1874 the Waters firm were making other craft from paper and shellac. One was the *Nautilus*, a canoe-like boat that could be paddled or rowed. It was a design by the Englishman, the Rev H. G. Baden-Powell (father of the founder of the Scout Movement) as a more roomy alternative to MacGregor's *Rob Roy*.

Nathaniel H. Bishop, of Tom's River, New Jersey, was a sportsman who had already gained fame by a hike across the continent and a voyage in a small boat down the Mississippi. In 1874 he took one of Water's paper boats (the *Maria Therasa*) and paddled and rowed it from Troy, New Tork, to Cedar Keys, Florida, a distance of something like 1.000 miles (1609km).

The route included streams, rivers and the open sea. Bishop abandoned sailing gear soon after starting and used paddles in narrow water and oars on open stretches. An early mishap was a capsize in the 16-mile (25km) wide Delaware Bay. The hull took a pounding on the oyster shell beach. Bishop said it was only scratched, but if he had been using a wooden canoe it would have been wrecked. At another point he capsized during a winter storm offshore. He swam to land and fortunately his boat was washed ashore and he retrieved most of his belongings, including a waterproof bag containing dry clothing and some brandy. This, appropriately, was Slaughter Bay.

Much of the route followed what is now the intra-coastal waterway, comparatively sheltered for larger yachts, but containing parts hazardous to Bishop's craft. The whole journey lasted five months and in that time the boat was never out of the water for more than three days.

It might have been thought that the future of these boats was assured, but the factory of Elisha Waters & Sons was completely destroyed by fire in 1876. The owners did not revive the business and would not part with their patents so the process languished.

First Oars Across the Atlantic
On 1 August, 1897, an 18ft (5.4m) rowing boat entered the harbour at St Marys, Isles of Scilly, after leaving New York on 6 June of the same year. With a crew of two she had covered 3,075 miles (4,949km) in 55 days, making an average of 56 miles (90km) per day. This was the *Richard K. Fox*, rowed by two American-Norwegians, George Harvo, aged 31, and Frank Samuelson, aged 26. These were the days before radio and confirmation of their achievement took a little time.

A doctor at St Marys examined the men and found them fit, except that Samuelson had sea boils on his hands. They continued up the English Channel to Le Havre, finishing their voyage there on 7 August.

The boat was a double-ender, 18ft (5.4m) long and 5ft (1.5m) beam, open throughout and planked with cedar. There were watertight compartments at each end, mainly stowed with food and water. A waterproof cover could be fitted over the boat, with apertures for the men to sit and continue to row. Everything in the boat was secured in case of capsize, and the keel had hand holes so that the men had something to grip if they had to right the boat. They catered for a crossing of 60 days, allowing 1 gal (4.5 litres) drinking water per day, and ample food. There is no record of what cooking arrangements they had, or their navigation arrangements, but they were adequate and they were capable navigators as they made a good landfall at the Bishop Rock lighthouse, off the Scillies.

The *Richard K. Fox* carried five pairs of oars, but there were no sails or other means of propulsion. The crew had the benefit of the prevailing wind, that would help them even without sails, but the boat was rowed almost continuously. During the day both men pulled pairs of oars. At night they stood 3½ hour watches, with one man rowing and one sleeping.

Ten days out from New York they spoke to German steamer *Fuerst Bismarck,* bound for New York. By then they were 500 miles (804km) on their way and refused help. On 1 July they made contact with a Nova Scotia fishing schooner, the *Leader* and went on board for a meal. On 7 July they started three days of gales and capsized. After a lot of effort they righted the boat and bailed her. They had lost some of their stores and one pair of oars, but they were able to continue rowing. After another five days they spoke to the Norwegian barque *Zito,* when they were just about halfway. They accepted some provisions and water.

For another nine days they just rowed steadily on, then they met another Norwegian barque, when they only had 400 miles (643km) to go.

At Le Havre the boat was exhibited, then the two men went by ferry to London and returned home by the steamer *Island.* The ship suffered from head winds all the way, and one story is that Harvo and Samuelson rowed their boat 200 miles (322km) to New York for assistance, but that was no more true than another tale that had them drown while rowing in the English Channel.

First Canoe Across the Atlantic
There is a belief that an Eskimo from Greenland arrived in his kayak on the west coast of Scotland. He had been washed off his course while hunting seals and had survived by catching fish and sucking moisture from them. He is said to have died soon after reaching Scotland. There is no proof that this trip took place and the first authenticated canoe crossing was that by Captain Romer (or Roemer).

Klepper, a German firm of canoe builders, had made a reputation as producers of the finest folding canoes, but they must have had doubts about the practicability of the project when they were asked to produce a canoe for crossing the Atlantic. The fabric-covered decked folding kayak-type craft they built was called the *Deutscher Sport* and was 21ft 6in (6.3m) long and 3ft (91cm) beam. The paddler was a German, Franz Romer.

Romer left Lisbon on 28 March, 1928, which was not the best time for a departure, according to modern thought on trans-Atlantic voyages. He got to Las Palmas, Canary Islands, 17 days later. Here he caught a fever, but was able to leave on 2 June. He spoke to several ships on the crossing and had difficulty in discouraging them from wanting to rescue him. After 58 days at sea he reached St Thomas, in the Virgin Islands. He had to be carried ashore as he had lost the use of his legs.

He spent six weeks at St Thomas. He wanted to reach the mainland at Florida. As this meant island-hopping with not more than 40 miles (64km) between islands he thought this would be easy, but he left on 12 September for Santo Domingo, but he was caught in a hurricane and was drowned.

Not many details of this trip are available, probably because Romer died before he was able to write about it. He must have had sail as well as paddle, but there could not have been much room to relax in his canoe. There might have been room to lie down after he had worked through some of his stores, but the only way to exercise his legs would have been to go over the side and swim.

Information published by the Klepper company is not very explicit, but they give the distance covered as 3,852 miles (6,199km) in 58 days, with an average of 56.6 miles (90km) per day and the best 24-hour period as 128 miles (205km). Romer was decorated with a gold medal by the American Governor W. Evans.

Cockleshell Heroes
In the early part of the 1939/45 war folding canoes of the types used for touring in and around Britain were examined and their possible use for military purposes considered. As a result folding two-seaters very little different in overall size were built for military purposes. They were much more substantially made, but their lines were much the same, with length around 17ft (5m) and beam just under 3ft (91cm). Inflatable bags along the gunwales gave extra stability and a service load could be up to two tons (2,000kg).

The canoes were designed to be carried in submarines and they could be passed out through torpedo tubes. They were used successfully for many operations in many parts of the world. A decked canoe can be paddled silently and unobtrusively so that it can penetrate enemy waters where other craft could not hope to go.

The most famous exploit was the sinking of enemy ships in Bordeaux Harbour by a party of marines under Major H. G. Hasler in 1942. This has been covered in a book and film with the title 'Cockleshell Heroes'—an apt name, but one not coined until after the war.

Bordeaux is 75 miles (120km) up the Gironde river, but armed merchant ships had been getting in and out and avoiding the British blockade. The problem was to sink some of these ships to block the harbour. The scheme adopted was to use canoes, slipped from a submarine 15 miles (24km) from the mouth of the river. They would be paddled up the river in four nights and they and their crews would be hidden during the day. Five two-seater canoes were used. A sixth was damaged in launching and scuttled beside the submarine.

Major Hasler had the front seat in the leading canoe and his mate was Marine Sparks. This was *Catfish*. After paddling through a tide rip off the river mouth one of the canoes and its crew were missing. While getting into the estuary through surf another canoe capsized and was damaged. The crew was got ashore and the canoe sunk, after its limpet mines had been transferred to the remaining three craft.

The remaining force of three canoes continued up the river. They did not make the progress they expected and had several close shaves with enemy patrol craft and enemy forces while they were hiding under nets amongst reeds ashore during the days. During one encounter with patrol boats, one canoe was shot at and the crew killed. The remaining two canoes avoided detection and continued.

Eventually these two canoes were taken right into Bordeaux and limpet mines attached to several ships. Their delayed action allowed the canoes to be got away before the explosions. The mission had succeeded. The canoes were scuttled and their crews landed to walk into occupied France. Only Major Hasler and Marine Sparks survived. They were helped by the French and got back to England via Spain five months later.

Inflatable Across the Atlantic
What amounted to a drift across the Atlantic in a small inflatable boat was successfully completed by Dr Alain Bombard. This Frenchman held the belief that man could live on what he could get from the sea. His way to prove it was to cross the Atlantic without food or water.

Dr Bombard had discovered that man can live on sea water for about two weeks, providing it is only taken in small quantities. He learned that the Polynesians mixed sea water with the juice squeezed from fish. The result was a de-salted drink that was quite palatable. We rely on sugar, but Dr Bombard investigated how Eskimos could live quite healthily without sugar. He concluded that 'The human organism can synthetise sugar from fats and proteins provided one drinks enough of them.' To get enough vitamins to combat scurvy he said, 'If one eats 100 grams of plankton a day there is no danger of scurvy.' Plankton can be collected in a small mesh net. So providing he could catch fish and collect plankton, his theory was that he could survive.

The boat was an inflatable lifesaving dinghy, basically the same as used today as a yacht tender. The inflatable tubes formed the sides and curved around to form the bow. There was a rigid bottom and a wooden transom, of the type intended to take an outboard motor. Of course, he was without a motor. He was really without any means of propulsion, except for a tiny sail, which would do little more than keep the boat headed away from the wind. He called this strange trans-Atlantic craft *l'Herétique*.

Bombard left Casablanca on 24 August, 1952, and got to Las Palmas in twelve days. He left there to drift towards the West Indies on 19 October, without water or food.

He had a surprisingly uneventful crossing. He had one narrow escape when he went into the sea to recover an air cushion blown overboard. He had let go his sea anchor, which was made of light material. Instead of dropping into the sea to stop the boat, it filled with air on the surface, so that the boat was blowing away at just about the same speed as Bombard could swim. He kept pace with the boat for about an hour, then the sea anchor became waterlogged and sank, so he was able to catch up and climb on board. By then he must have been in a very weak state.

He only spoke to one ship—the British *Arakara*—and went on board for a light meal and to radio home. He was then 700 miles (1,126km) from his destination. He got to Bridgetown, Barbados twelve days later, after sixty-five days at sea and a crossing of nearly 3,000 miles (4,828km).

He had proved his point. Except for the one meal, he had lived on what he could get from the sea. As a result of this he showed that a castaway could live off the sea if he knew how, but he concluded that there were more important things contributing to survival: 'All shipwreck survivors can escape death provided that they can surmount, in order of importance, despair, fatigue, thirst and hunger.'

Canoe Twice Across the Atlantic

Dr Hannes Lindemann (a German) worked in Liberia for an American rubber firm. He obtained a dug-out canoe, 23ft 6in (59m) long and 2ft 6in (76cm) beam, which he fitted with cork sponsons for stability. He fitted a tiny cabin and gave the canoe a gaff sloop rig. In this he sailed across the Atlantic from Las Palmas on 26 October, 1955. He reached the Virgin Islands on 28 December, then went on to Haiti. He finally gave this boat to President Tubman of Liberia.

Of course, that voyage was under sail and the boat (the *Liberia II*), despite its origin and narrow beam, might be considered more of a yacht. However, Lindemann, who was a doctor of medicine, only made that crossing to get experience of the trade winds, in preparation for another crossing to be made in a genuine canoe.

He bought a standard two-seat folding Klepper canoe, of the type known as 'Aerius' with built-in air bags inside the gunwales. It was 17ft 4in (5m) long, about 3ft (91cm) beam and weighed 60lb (27kg). It was a standard Klepper product as available to anyone and not specially built or adapted. He called it *Liberia III*.

This was the time when catamarans were beginning their modern developments and when Lindemann shipped his canoe to Las Palmas in preparation for the crossing, he was met by James Wharram, a leading catamaran sailor and designer, of considerable experience. Wharram got to know Lindemann. He said that at first he was convinced that

Lindemann did not stand a chance of crossing, but as he got to know him and observed his training and preparations, he thought that by the time he left his chances were 50/50.

Lindemann trained at Las Palmas by swimming and canoeing several miles each day. He also practiced Yoga, although he would not use that name and talked of 'Autogenes Training.' He trained himself to go without proper sleep. He would be unable to lie down and had to relax while sitting. He carried milk and beer instead of water.

The canoe was given a crude outrigger. This was at Wharram's suggestion and mainly so that Lindemann could perform his natural functions. Besides paddles, there was a small sail. Stowage of sufficient equipment and stores must have been quite a problem, and getting at items stowed under the decks towards the ends, must have called for some contortions in anything of a sea.

Lindemann left Las Palmas on 20 October, 1956, and crossed in November, December and January. These are the months when the trade winds are strong. Romer had crossed in June and July, when they are comparatively light. In the strong winds Lindemann capsized three times, losing some of his stores. He retained a fishing speargun, and the use of this enabled him to get enough food to supplement what was left and keep going.

Liberia III reached St Martin, Leeward Islands, 76 days after setting out. Unlike Romer, who had to be carried ashore, Lindemann was able to walk up steps on to the quay. By then he was 50lb (22kg) lighter.

Modern Oarsmen Across the Atlantic

Captain John Ridgway and Sergeant Chay Blyth, both of the Parachute Regiment, had

had an adventurous service life and had competed together in the Devizes-Westminster canoe race. Ridgway had spent a few months in the Merchant Navy. Blyth had never been to sea. Looking for something adventurous to do, they decided to row the Atlantic. They bought a standard Yorkshire dory, 20ft (6m) long, which had not found a buyer at the London Boat Show, and shipped it to America.

At Cape Cod local fishermen suggested a few modifications and provided some ash oars, but basically this was an open boat, double-ended, with a narrow flat bottom and flared sides, to which had been added some plastic foam buoyant end decks. They called her *English Rose III*. The boat and her crew represented a set-up not vastly different from the *Richard K. Fox* crossing in 1897.

This was 1966, when another pair of British oarsmen were also planning to row across in a specially-built boat, called *Puffin*. David Johnstone and John Hoare left Boston on 20 May, 1966. There was news of them about 750 miles (1,200km) from Land's End in August, but on 15 October a frigate of the Royal Canadian Navy found *Puffin* afloat, but capsized and abandoned.

Ridgway and Blyth left Cape Cod on 4 June, 1966. They divided the crossing into three parts. The first was the 300 mile (480km) crossing of the Labrador current, during which they rowed 12 hours together and allowed for both sleeping eight hours, while the boat lay to a sea anchor. This took them to the edge of the Gulf Stream, when they planned to still do 12 hours together during the day, then alternate in two-hour watches throughout the night. The third phase started in mid-Atlantic, when they expected to make contact with Shackleton aircraft of RAF Coastal Command. This worked out much as they had planned, except there was no contact with aircraft.

At first they were very cramped, until they had eaten their way through some of the stores. They sat on fixed thwarts, which gave trouble with soreness. When only 150 miles (240km) out they experienced the edge of a hurricane and had to throw away food damaged by sea water.

As this crossing was through the North Atlantic shipping lanes, they contacted several ships, but usually only checked bearings and asked to be reported.

In mid-Atlantic they experienced a five-day storm. There was no room to relax properly and they had to shelter under a canvas sheet while sitting across the bottom of the boat. As there was no self-bailing arrangement, water that came on board had to be pumped out by hand. Ridgway spent some of the time teaching Blyth French!

After 92 days they arrived at Aran Island off the west coast of Ireland. They had rowed about 3,500 miles (5,633km) in a quarter of a year, living in an open space about 12ft (3.6m) by 5ft (1.5m). The last man to speak to them as they left America was a priest named Father McMahon. As they landed on Aran they were greeted by another priest, who introduced himself as Father McMahon.

Alone Across the Atlantic

The two-man attempted crossings of the Atlantic, one successful and the other a disaster, in 1966, were both from west to east, but in 1969 John Fairfax set out alone to row from east to west. He succeeded in crossing from the Canary Islands to Florida in 180 days.

The boat used—*Britannia*—was designed

by the late Uffa Fox, famous for many successful yachts and other craft. She was built by Clare Lallow, of Cowes. As was necessary for a boat to be propelled by one man, the lines had to be easily driven, but the hull was given a stable round-bottomed form, with not much freeboard amidships, to allow for the oars, but an internal floor sloped slightly towards the centreline, and enclosed watertight compartments. At the ends were inflatable shelters, something like the ends of lifeboats. These gave self-righting qualities and provided some minimal shelter. Slots in the bottom allowed a rudder to be used and gave alternative positions for a daggerboard to act as a keg and aid directional control. Water coming over the sides ran out through the slots.

Britannia was 25ft (6.3m) long, with very little overhang, being 24ft (6.1m) on the waterline. Experience with this boat obviously influenced the design of *Britannia II (see next section)*, which was given considerable overhang. The beam was 4ft 9in (1.40m). Uffa Fox followed his successful wartime designs for airborne lifeboats.

John Fairfax did much of his training rowing a hired boat on the Serpentine, in London's Hyde Park.

Britannia was shipped to Las Palmas in the Canary Islands. After a brief stay there, sorting and loading stores, John Fairfax left on 20 January, 1969, heading for Florida, 3,600 miles (5,800km) away by the shortest route. He allowed for about 4,000 miles (6,400km) and was about right.

Besides some fresh water in plastic containers, there was a distilling plant. Radio sufficient to give two-way communication all the way was provided, as part of a deal with a newspaper, which had rights in the story.

Early progress was disappointing, with westerly winds. Rowing more than 12 hours only resulted in less than 20 miles real progress per day. Contact was made with several ships and Fairfax went on board a few briefly. By mid-March Fairfax began to experience calms and winds from directions other than west, so progress improved. Many fish were caught, mainly by spearing.

Fairfax reported remaining fit for two months, then he had to begin treating a rash on his seat. His hands did not suffer, but he wore gloves most of the time. Later he bruised a leg, but otherwise remained fit. When 98 days out *Britannia* was almost rammed and sunk by a ship misguidedly coming to her aid.

As the radio worked satisfactorily most of the time, Fairfax was in touch with the shore and his position was known, so there were no long gaps without news. This also meant that as he neared America, planes and boats with press and TV men knew where to find him. He rowed *Britannia* on to a beach at Miami at 1.45 p.m. on 19 July, 1969, 180 days after setting out, giving an average rate of progress of just under 25 miles (40km) per day. He had experienced high winds, but no real gales and had a comparatively uneventful crossing.

Rowing Across the Pacific
After his rowing exploit across the Atlantic John Fairfax looked for more seas to conquer and prepared to tackle the much greater distance involved in rowing across the Pacific from San Francisco, 8,000 miles (13,000km) to Australia. His Atlantic experience had given him very definite ideas about how this was to be done and the sort of boat he needed.

The boat, *Britannia II*, was also designed by the late Uffa Fox. It was about 36ft (11m) long, but much of this was taken up by long overhanging ends. On the waterline it was about 27ft (8m). Beam was just over 5ft (1.6m). The centre section was a very stable broad D form, but there was quite a rapid taper towards the ends. A rudder was slung underneath and could be withdrawn. There was provision for two drop keels similar to those used on dinghies. The boat was sealed by a deck at seating level, with storage below. At the ends were large buoyant plastic blisters, like those on coastal life-boats. Enough buoyancy was built-in to make the boat unsinkable and the ends were intended to right the boat after a capsize. The two oarsmen had sliding seats, as used on racing craft. The boat would bail itself through the centreboard and rudder slots. *Britannia II* was built of double-planked mahogany at the yard of Clare Lallow of Cowes, launched there, then shipped to San Francisco.

Fairfax's partner was a girl, Sylvia Cook, with some racing rowing experience, but with no knowledge of seagoing. She had helped him with office work and his preliminary planning for the solo Atlantic crossing. One preparation was to build up their weight by eating before starting, so as to allow for the loss of weight expected on the voyage. Some shelter was provided by crawling under the end blisters. Cooking had to be done there or in the open.

Some time was spent at the start getting food and equipment. As little money was available suppliers had to be persuaded to donate items, as far as possible. Water capacity was 90 gallons (350 litres). This was replenished on the way. Food was also replenished by fishing and at calling places.

After some false starts, *Britannia II* got away from San Francisco on 26 April, 1971. A call was made at Ensenda, south of Los Angeles. This was left on 3 June and the course showed an erratic line on the chart until they reached Washington Island in mid-Pacific on 6 October, 1971. They stayed there until 12 November. They had Christmas at sea and made the island of Onotoa in the Gilbert group on 9 January, 1972, but when landing through the breakers the bottom of the boat was stove in. Fortunately there were boatyard facilities at Tarawa, another island in the group, and they were able to get away with a repaired boat on 7 February.

The rowing schedule was about thirteen hours a day, with John Fairfax doing eight hours and Sylvia Cook five hours. On 28 February they met a cargo ship, the *Tri-Ellis* and were able to get fresh fruit and send messages. They had their own radio, but did not have much success in operating it.

John Fairfax was a keen underwater swimmer and he succeeded in catching many fish to supplement their diet. His companion could not swim. When about nine-tenths of the way to Australia, John Fairfax received a serious bite on the arm by a shark, while he was in the water. They used what first-aid knowledge they had and tried to contact ships seen for help, but without success. With drift and Sylvia rowing occasionally they approached the Great Barrier Reef and experienced the edge of a cyclone. Fortunately the arm healed enough for John to begin to share the work.

Eventually they reached Haymen Island, off the Queensland coast, where they met civilization and completed their voyage on 22 April, 1972, nearly a year after setting out.

GLOSSARY

The language of the sea has produced a very large number of words, many of which have found their way into ordinary use, while others have become obsolete. The meanings of a selection of words that may be of value to readers of this book are given below. Where the meaning is peculiar to a particular branch of small boating this is shown by 'C' for canoeing, 'D' for dinghies and pleasure boating, 'R' for racing rowing craft. Meanings which are unmarked are applicable to most types of boating.

Abaft	Behind or to the stern
Abeam	To the side
Aft	Towards the stern
Amidships	The middle of the boat
Astern	Behind the boat
Athwart	Across the boat
Back	Stop progress or drive boat backwards
Best boat	The finest racing craft available (R)
Blade	The flat part of an oar or paddle
Bow	Forward part of the boat
Bow board	Transom at forward end of a pram dinghy (D)
Bow side	The side which the bow oar extends (R)
Bum boat	Boat from shore serving a ship
Button	Leather disc (R) or quadrant locating against rowlock
Carry	Main part of stroke (R)
Carvel	A method of planking, using strips laid fore and aft, to give a flush surface
Catamaran	A twin-hulled boat
Catch	Beginning of stroke (R)
Chine, chinse	An angle between sides and bottom of a hull
Clench	Less-common name for clinker
Clinker	A method of planking, with strips fore and aft, lapped over each other
Clogs	Leather boots, part of stretcher (R)
Coaming	The board around a cockpit
Coble	Beach boat, particularly on Yorkshire coast
Cockpit	Opening in decked boat, alternative to well
Corinthian	Victorian name for amateur
Crab	Inability to extract oar from water, usually due to slicing too deep (R)
Crutch	Alternative name for rowlock

Cutter	A large double-banked transom-sterned pulling boat	Helm	Steering arrangements
		Inboard	Within the boat
Davit	Type of crane for raising and lowering a boat from a ship	Kayak	Decked double-ended craft propelled with double-bladed paddle (C)
Dinghy	General name for a small boat, originally a tender to a yacht	Keel	The central outside member of a hull
		Keelson	Internal part of keel
Dory	Flat-bottomed, flair-sided sea boat	Knee	Angle bracket in boat construction, usually wooden
Double chine	A hull with two chines at each side	Knot	Nautical mile per hour
		Lapstrake	Alternative name for clinker, more common in America
Double diagonal	Planking with two skins laid diagonally to the keel and crossing each other		
		Larboard	Early name for Starboard
Fan	Old name for blade of canoe paddle	Launch	The principal boat of a ship. Today: a power boat
Feather	Having the oar blade parallel with the water when in the air	Leather	Protected part of oar where it fits in rowlock
		Leeward	(pronounced 'looard') Away from the wind
Fixed tub	Boxlike boat fixed to bank, often with mirror, for training (R)	Long boat	Large ship's boat, usually with eight or ten oars
Freeboard	Height of gunwale above waterline	Loom	Shaft of oar or paddle, specifically the inboard part
Funny	Early double-ended sculling wager boat		
		Montague whaler	Five-oared Naval boat
Garboard strake	Plank next to the keel	Moulded plywood	Hull built from strips of veneer glued diagonally in several layers
Gate	Metal piece to prevent oar lifting from rowlock (R)		
	Hanging pair of poles to be negotiated in slalom (C)	Muffle	Quieten oars with cloth at the rowlocks
Gig	Open ship's boat with several pairs of oars	Neck	The shaft of an oar between blade and leather
Grip	Handle end of an oar		
Gunwale	The upper edge at the side of a hull	Outboard	Outside the boat
		Outrigger	see Rigger
Hard chine	A hull with an angle	Paddle	Rowing slowly (R)
Heave-to	Bring the boat head to wind		Blade used when facing forward (C)

Painter	Rope attached to bow and used for mooring (D)	Rowing	A boat pulled by a crew with one or more men per oar (R)
Peter boat	Small beamy double-end boat, particularly used on Thames for fishing	Rowlock	Notch in side of boat (Royal Navy) or metal fitting to take oar at side of boat
Port	The left side facing forward	Saxboard	Wood on gunwale to carry riggers
Praam	Scandinavian craft with bottom planking swept up to gunwale line (D)	Scull	Smaller oar, two being used by one man (R)
Pram	A dinghy with a transom at the bow, instead of a pointed stem (D)	Seamanship	Knowledge of boats and the sea. Comparable to 'Watermanship'
Proa	Pacific sailing canoe. Malaysian boat	Sheer	Line of deck or gunwale when viewed from side
Punt	Flat-bottomed river craft Propelling the craft with a pole Alternative name for a dinghy in some parts (D)	Shell	Very light boat, made of one thin layer of wood (R)
		Skiff	Light open river rowing boat (D)
Quant	Use a pole to push on the bottom. The pole used for this	Slalom	Whitewater contest, in which canoeists negotiate obstacle 'gates' (C)
Randan	A boat rowed by three men, with the centre one having a pair of oars and the others one each	Sliding seat	Seat on runners to allow oarsman to stretch and bend legs (R)
Recovery	Returning the oar for another stroke (R)	Span	Distance from centre of seat to thole pins, in rowing boat (R)
Regatta	Competitive rowing event —originally Italian		Distance between thole pins in sculling boat (R)
Ribs	Crosswise structure of a boat	Starboard	Right side looking forward
Rigger	Struts extending from side of boat to carry rowlocks (R)	Stem	The upright member at the forward point of a boat
		Stern	The aft end of any boat
Rocker	Keel-line curved up towards ends	Sternpost	Upright member at the stern of a double-ended craft
Round-bottomed	Hull with rounded cross-sections	Strake	Lengthwise plank of a boat's skin
Runner	Metal rail on which sliding seat travels (R)	Stretcher	Footrest

Stroke	The sternmost oarsman (R) The force used to propel a rowing boat	Tub pair or four	Heavy clinker boats for training (R)
Stroke side	The side on which the stroke oar extends (R)	Veer	Change direction. Let rope run out
Stringer	Lengthwise member inside hull	Wager boat	Early racing boat (R)
Sweep	Large oar, often used for steering	Wale	Extra strake at gunwale
		Washboard	Less common name for coaming
Tender	A boat used to service a larger craft	Watermanship	Knowledge of boats and water—usually inland and comparable to 'Seamanship' for seagoing boatmen
Thole	The vertical side of the rowlock against which the oar is pulled (R) Thole pins are a pair of pegs in the gunwale to serve as rowlock (D)	Well	Part of boat not decked, alternative to cockpit
		Wet-bob	A rowing man
		Whaler	A boat used for whaling. Five-oared Naval boat
Thwart	Plank seat across boat (D). All of the seating equipment (R)	Wherry	General purpose boats used by watermen
Tiller	Handle to control a rudder	Whiff	Early outrigged sculling boat (R)
Timbers	Alternative name for rib	Whitewater	Fast-flowing river with rapids (C)
Tingle	A wood or metal patch on a hull		
Toothpick	Fine sculling boat	Windward	Towards the wind
Toss oars	Hold oars vertically in boat as salute	Yaw	Swing from side to side
		Yoke	Cross-piece at head of rudder, used with rope yoke lines
Treenails	Wood pegs joining parts of boat together		
Trim	The level of a boat	Zephyr	Light breeze Vest or singlet (R)
Trimaran	Three-hulled vessel		

BIBLIOGRAPHY

A large number of books contain references to small craft, usually incidental to other matters, but the following books are some which should prove useful to anyone wanting to read more about boats of the types mentioned in this book.

Alone at Sea, Dr Hannes Lindemann, Random House, USA.

The Bark Canoes and Skin Boats of North America, Adney and Chapelle, Smithsonian Institution, USA. 1964.

British Coracles and Irish Curraghs, James Hornell, Society for Nautical Research. 1938.

Clinker Boatbuilding, John Leather, Granada Publishing. 1973.

Cockleshell Heroes, C. E. Lucas Phillips, William Heinemann. 1956.

The Life-boat Story, Patrick Howarth, Routledge & Kegan Paul.

Men, Ships and the Sea, National Geographic Society, USA.

Oars Across the Pacific, John Fairfax and Sylvia Cook, William Kimber. 1972.

A Thousand Miles in the Rob Roy Canoe, J. MacGregor, reprint of 1880 edition by British Canoe Union. 1963.

Working Watercraft, Thomas C. Gillmer, Patrick Stephens. 1973.

INDEX